Author: Gary L. Richardson

The Second in *The Verdict Is In Series*—

Thank God.
They Ate the Apple!

With Tom Westbrook

InstantPublisher.com

All scripture quotations used are NIV unless otherwise noted, and are taken from the Holy Bible, New International Version© Copyright © 1973, 1978, 1984 by International Bible Society. Used by permission of Zondervan Publishing House. All rights reserved.

Scripture quotations marked KJV are taken from The King James Version of the Bible.

Scripture quotations marked NAS are taken from the New American Standard Bible. Copyright © The Lockman Foundation 1960, 1962, 1963, 1968, 1971, 1972, 1973, 1975, 1977. Used by permission.

Scripture quotations marked NKJV are taken from The New King James Version of the Bible. Copyright © 1979, 1980, 1982, Thomas Nelson, Inc.

Scripture quotations marked THE MESSAGE are from The Message: The Bible in Contemporary Language, copyright © 2002 by Eugene H. Peterson. All rights reserved. Used by permission of NavPress Publishing Group.

Verses marked TLB are taken from The Living Bible © 1971. Used by permission of Tyndale House Publishers, Inc., Wheaton, Illinois 60189. All rights reserved.

Thank God, They Ate The Apple
Printed in the United States of America. All rights reserved under International Copyright Law. Contents and/or cover may not be reproduced in whole or in part in any form without the express written consent of the Publisher.

ISBN 978-1-60458-306-9

Copyright © 2008 by Gary L. Richardson: All Rights
Tulsa, Oklahoma
Web site: www.GaryRichardsonSpeaks.com   E-mail: glrichardson@rlfok.com

Published by
InstantPublisher.com

Front Cover Design: Jill Westbrook, Firefrost Studios 2008.

Books by Gary Richardson:
Conversations on Faith
The Verdict Is In: Fear Is Never Your Friend
And coming soon —
The Verdict Is In: Black Robe Fever

Table of Contents

	Page
Foreword — Wade Burleson	5
Acknowledgements	9
Introduction	11
Let this book talk to you — Tom Westbrook	15
What This Book is Not	17
1 Learning to Examine the Evidence — *God's Word*	19
2 Unlearning and Letting Go	35
3 Why Live with Regret and Shame, When We Can Dance?	51
4 It's All About Him. (I.A.A.H.)	69
5 LIMITS on GOD? — *You're Kidding Me!*	87
6 God Asks None of Us To Rescue His Reputation — *When the World Explodes*	101
7 God Asks None of Us To Rescue His Reputation — *When He Works in Someone*	115
8 God Asks None of Us To Rescue His Reputation — *When It Feels Personal.*	127
9 God Asks None of Us To Rescue His Reputation — *When He is Transforming The World.*	135
10 God-Tools for You — *He Wastes Nothing*	147
11 The E. R. — *Embrace & Renew*	179
12 The Bold Frontier: Beyond "Scary" Things — *Living in God's Plan For Our Lives*	205

4

FOREWORD

"Let your religion be less of a theory and more of a love affair." G.K. Chesterton

As a follower of Jesus Christ who has devoted his life to help assist and encourage others who belong to the Chief Shepherd, I have sometimes observed that the Lord's flock, as we wander through life's journey with God, will often find our comfort in one of two different kinds of religious pastures.

First, many us view Christianity as a set of rules and regulations that God passed down to us. Our perceived relationship with this cosmic Lawgiver is based on the feelings we attribute to Him as He watches us either obey — or disobey — His commands. We will often measure His enjoyment of us by the good feelings we have about ourselves when we 'measure up' to His standards, or the guilt we bear when we fail to meet His Law. Some well-meaning sheep will even walk with us in our journey and add to our burden by whispering heavy pronouncements of what is required of us to be worthy of our Chief Shepherd's blessings. Walking these 'paths of righteousness' becomes such a burden that we soon succumb to the weariness of never being able to please our heavenly Father. In time, our spirits are so filled with the "do's and don'ts" of religion, the searing sense of the soul's sin, and the gutsy guilt of simply living a human life that we give up trying to measure up. The favor and approval of God seems so far out of reach that we lie down in the religious pasture land of

God's flock with other hurting sheep that are burned out and worn out.

It is precisely at this time in our lives that our Chief Shepherd will 'lead us beside still waters' to the second kind of religious pasture. He will bring into our lives those in His flock, including some under shepherds (pastors and teachers), who have learned what it means to rest in the Chief Shepherd. They will help lead us to understand and accept God's sovereignty over, and purpose in, each of our lives. We will be led to drink from the deep and still streams of truth that reflects Christianity as being all about God — not us.

We will see God displayed in all His majesty, His faithfulness, His power, His love, and His mercy. We will be refreshed to learn that everything that happens in our lives, even our sins and failures, are part of His purposes and plans. We will experience religion, like Chesterton exhorts, as 'less of a theory and more of a love affair.'

Gary Richardson is one of those under shepherds that the Lord may use to lead you to those 'still waters.' The book you hold in your hand, *Thank God They Ate the Apple*, is a culmination of years of thought and Bible study that has led the author to drink deeply from the river of God's sovereignty. For some followers of Christ, the conclusions of this book may be shocking, but for many of you who have trusted Christ and experienced the shattered dreams of an unanticipated life, the self-doubt of an underperforming life, and the guilt of an 'out of control' personal life — you will find something incredibly revealing about God in this book: 'The Master won't ever walk out and fail to return. If He works severely, He also works tenderly. His stockpiles of loyal love are immense." In other words, you will fall in love with God because of who He is, not because of who you are.

Author Gary Richardson is not a theologian by trade and he acknowledges this fact. He is an attorney. Like 'The Prince of Preachers,' Charles Spurgeon, who himself had no formal theological training, Gary Richardson has learned of God while on his knees, through personal study of Scriptures and by simply being a keen observer of life. Gary is also a wonderful storyteller. He will take the profound, eternal biblical truth of God's sovereignty, and apply it to the home and to the heart.

Some Christians object to God's absolute control because they believe if all the things that occurred in their lives were under the direct supervision of God, then He would be nothing but a severe ogre who loved pain. Gary will show you through impeccable logic, an abundance of Scripture, and captivating stories that God's plan is always 'beautiful.' It is a word that you will read over and over again in this book — 'beautiful.' If you do not yet understand how your sin, how your failure, how your mistakes can ultimately be considered 'beautiful' by God, then this book is your map to the discovery of those still waters.

When the Apostle Paul instructed the Romans about the sovereignty and grace of God, he came to a time when he anticipated an objection. He knew that some would say to him, "Paul, if I believed what you are saying, that God's grace is such that my sin *always* works out for good and ultimately fulfills a beautiful plan that God has for my life, then I would simply say "I am going to keep on sinning!" Anticipating this objection, Paul asks the question, "What shall we say then? Shall we go on sinning that grace may increase?" Paul's answer to his own question in the Greek is *me genoito,* which is translated in some versions – "God forbid!"[1] Interestingly, the name for God is not in the Greek. The better translation would be 'Certainly not!' In other

---

[1] Romans 6:1

words, Paul tells us there are reasons he could give why we should turn from our sin, but the truth that he has already articulated remains irrefutable – our sin and our failure only ultimately fulfill the beautiful plan of God for our lives. That, my friend, is grace. And, you are never truly preaching grace until some people begin to object that you are giving license to sin. If that is the conclusion of some regarding this book, then you place the author in good company with the Apostle Paul.

Maybe you have made some very poor choices in secret that have now been discovered. Perhaps you have been arrested for a crime. Are you plagued with lingering doubt and guilt over a 'wasted' life? My prayer is that you will read *Thank God They Ate The Apple* and realize that real religion is a relationship with the God of all grace who will turn your sin and mistakes into the fulfillment of His beautiful purpose for your life.

Wade Burleson Pastor,
Enid, Oklahoma
February, 2008

ACKNOWLEDGMENTS

My deepest thanks...

My father, W. R. (Bill) Richardson. My father gave me such a security in his love that I could never rest until I knew my Heavenly Father's security for us all. Searching for God's security for me brought me to God's sovereignty.

Lanna. You are God's most precious lady to me. You have blessed me with your kindness, patience, and encouragement to devote the time for this project. Thanks for making the late nights on the computer bearable, and always being supportive.

David Willets. Thank you, pastor, for letting us walk through when your world exploded as you found God's sovereignty and peace in such a dark place!

Tom Westbrook. God found Tom, whose faith, experience, and education only sharpened his hunger for more Truth from God's Word. After months of calls, emails and visits, Tom said, "Let's get started." Repeatedly, he saw God's message to me in His word as I searched for Truth. Tom wrestled most with unlearning how any "free will" for a Christian is surrendered to God's Plan on experiencing salvation. He thinks you will have struggle there, too, unless God has already brought you to that place. Thank you, Tom, for keeping on keeping on. God Bless.

Jill Westbrook. What talent. Jill did the cover. It's so beautiful. Thank you, Jill.

Bob Baxter. God used my dear friend of over twenty years to bring Tom and me together.

Wade Burleson. What a giant, when it comes to the subject of Sovereignty. Thanks, Wade, for the conversations and the confirmations. Thanks for the foreword.

My Monday morning 7 AM study group. You guys are special. I have treasured our thirteen years together on Mondays. You have been a great sounding board for me.

Everyone: family members, friends, and enemies, who God used to do His work in me. The love, blessings, lessons, or challenges God brought to me through you are everything to me.

INTRODUCTION

When you write your story it feels simple to write until you start.

But it's not as hard as living your story.

Gary's story starts with an honest, good kid raised in a Christian home to enjoy successes. In school, athletics, business and church he excelled — but it was not enough. No achievement was ever enough.

In Gary's first book in the series, *The Verdict Is In: Fear is Never Your Friend,* he vulnerably, poignantly told us how we need courage to live, but courage was not enough to live *fully*. Hungers stalked him, needs drove him, and ghosts. Ghosts left him hollow, questing, questioning. You probably know those ghosts.

This book's first chapters simply unfold Gary's rise to success in sales and transition to trial law, but those don't encompass his story. His needs and cravings drove his story. Some needs granted him success, and some cravings ushered in shame and guilt that Gary learned to put behind him, and so can you.

Gary desperately desired what success, family and religion had not fulfilled. As he searched some wrong places and still succeeded wildly, he began hunting something larger and stronger than his desires — truth. Beyond knowledge, wisdom, and skill, Gary hungered for Truth and found that Truth has a Name.

He collected truth bits to find that each bit of Truth called him to go against what he had learned as a child. Truth often went against his indoctrination by his church and its college. And Truth was jealous: allowing no other lovers, no half-truths. As other truth contenders tried staking claims to his heart — Truth withered them with its piercing light, and pushed him to make his choice — always the same choice: Truth or less.

Truth has a Name and some people think He's been dead or at least irrelevant for a long time. Gary found Truth alive and uncompromising, yet willing to unlock anything to anyone who fearlessly seeks Him. Truth has a beautiful plan for all who seek Him, as you will learn.

Truth's Name is the Name above all names — the Lamb slain from before the world's foundations were laid.

Telling Gary's story is like dropping gifts on your doorstep. Some gifts in this book will encourage you. Some will alarm you. All will push you to leave your comfort zone to think, to believe, and even to act more courageously than you ever dared hope possible. But these gifts only work for you when you pick them up and bring them into "your house."

You know how you eat at a great restaurant and after an amazing meal; a waiter brings out that dessert tray? When you only read the desserts from a menu, they are just names someone dreamed up and wrote out on the menu. But when they sit on the tray in front of you chilled and beautiful, they hold a stronger, clearer appeal. The dessert tray is now in front of you.

If you are reading this, you have sat through many meals, some fantastic, and many promising more than they delivered. You have attended seminars, services, and teaching and hoped they could give what you believe existed. This book opens more than it promises.

Gary found these truth bits leading to Truth. They aren't controversial, but many people will find them daunting. Go ahead and argue with the words, not to stay safely where you are dying slowly but to see if they hold truth bits, or more amazingly — Truth.

You are eternally secure when you trust your life in Christ's salvation.

If you are blessed, you will be unlearning all of your life, and replacing half-truths or lies with Truth. Unlearning is scary. It's hard. Learning then displaces the less-than-the-best stuff with the Best.

The universe is All About God and not about you. Ouch. Put a Band-Aid on it and get on with life.

God is sovereign, chief, boss, dictator, CEO, Creator, and is not up for re-election — and He has proven that to you in three ways.

One, God is sovereign because He has a beautiful plan for your life — and if He is not absolutely and completely sovereign — He can't deliver on His promise to complete the astonishing work He began in each believer from the first day that he acknowledged Christ as Lord until he or she stands before Him, complete, transformed, and beautiful; but we are getting ahead of ourselves.

Two, God is sovereign because He created you with all your needs, hungers and cravings — whether they led you to God or led you to sin.

Three, God sent Jesus. Wow. He sent Jesus, part of Himself, Son. He sent Jesus to you. God is sovereign because He sent Truth to you. Oh, Truth's Name is Jesus, and ultimately Truth is not things we learn, it's — well, read on.

Enjoy Gary's story, and it could be that parts of his story will be your next chapter in your story.

14

LET THIS BOOK TALK TO YOU —

Bob Baxter called to ask if I would be interested in working on a book with his friend of twenty years, Gary. Bob's an ordained minister so I was intrigued when he said, "The idea is very novel, but his method is even more novel."

I was cautiously optimistic. This would be new to me, and I had already met a lifetime full of theological dabblers when pursuing my degrees.

I drove down to spend the night with Bob and Laura at their stunning ranch where Gene Autry spent boyhood summers, and Gary joined us for dinner and late night conversation. We sparred, no holds barred over his newfound discoveries from God's Word. We must have jousted twenty rounds out under the stars and enjoyed it. I found out two things under those cool stars.

One, Gary fears nothing — and that kept him from getting his feelings hurt as I pushed him hard on the thoughts you find in this book.

Two, Gary had found a way to talk about God's sovereignty that is missing in our churches — *and the world is starving for what we're missing.*

I laughed to think that God had given so much to a cigar smoking trial lawyer! Then I remembered I had plenty of company. People repeatedly missed what a carpenter from Nazareth was sent from God to show us.

I said yes and received from Gary, Bob's "novel idea at working on a book" — a nine-inch stack of emails! Gary's wrestling, his openness to hold to the Bible at any cost began chiseling away at many of my incomplete, untested ideas.

Reading through that stack took me through Gary's late-night exchanges with friends, enquirers and scoffers where he asked, questioned, and formulated — always relentlessly hungering for God's Truth — neither attacking nor being threatened by those that didn't see what God had shown him. What God showed me slowly. What God wants to show you.

It's hard to categorize this book. *Theological odyssey* comes to mind and at the end you will find yourself, welcomed home to a place you've never been before. Truly Home in God's love for you.

Enjoy. Argue. Laugh and rant, but read to the end. I'm forever glad I did.

Tom Westbrook, Spring, 2008

tom@connectionsite.org

WHAT THIS BOOK IS NOT

This is no theological treatise, but it explores what God's Word says fearlessly.

This is not an attempt to agree with some, and disagree with others. This is what I have found so far. God has been taking me beyond what I thought I knew all of my life: this is subject to change. If we agree, wow. If we disagree, that happens to all of us. I have some people with whom I disagree listed. No malice intended. Truth doesn't come in infinite flavors. Either someone is preaching Truth, or not.

This is not a syrupy autobiography. My life has rough edges, deep abysses, and nasty potholes — none of which is as important as God's overriding love and forgiveness.

This is not a rant.

This book does not claim to have all the answers, save one. As God continues His work in you, you find yourself more fearlessly surrendering to Him. Then you begin to see — He has never left you alone or on your own. He continues His work in you to fulfill His beautiful plan: the one He created your life to fulfill. He won't leave you alone or unchanged. Period.

Still growing fearless.

Gary L. Richardson, February 26, 2008.

1

LEARNING TO EXAMINE THE EVIDENCE: GOD'S WORD

If there were such a [perfectly Christian] society and you or I visited it, I think we should come away with a curious impression . . . Each of us would like some bits of it, but I am afraid very few of us would like the whole thing. That is just what one would expect if Christianity is the total plan for the human machine. We have all departed from that total plan in different ways, and each of us wants to make out that his own modification of the original plan is the plan itself. You will find this again and again about anything that is really Christian: everyone is attracted by bits of it and wants to pick out those bits and leave the rest.

-C. S. Lewis from *Mere Christianity*

Hebrews 4:12 (NASB) the Word of God is living and active and sharper than any two-edged sword, and piercing as far as the division of soul and spirit, of both joints and marrow, and able to judge the thoughts and intentions of the heart.

Where I started into adulthood and my questions that left me empty may be very different than where you started. Just the same, you have found questions that left you empty, or they found you. I start with my story, because God used my story to answer my emptiness.

I Learned Sin While Being Faithful in Church.

My family's weekly rhythms ebbed and flowed around church: Sunday, mornings and nights; Wednesday nights; revivals; Vacation Bible School; camps.

My father first 'went to church' when courting my mother. Almost immediately he joined the church and laid his cigarettes aside, having already escaped the heavy drinking in his home. He quit. With only a third grade education Dad became a self-trained preacher, handsome, and radiating a great personality. People were drawn to him. He was a great man, my hero.

Dad wasn't demanding about church things, maybe because I was already sincere, maybe because he didn't grow up in church in all the rules. Dad's Biblical education came from reading the Bible, not manuals or texts. When my church friends had to miss school activities and ball games to attend a revival, Dad never required me to do that. Our church was against dances, movies, and all sorts of possible evils, but Dad didn't major on those things. Mom did. She worked to make us good, to make us different from other, worldly friends at school.

My twin sister, Rheda, and I found a refuge from being different from our 'school' friends: we were outstanding athletes. Every year our school elected a Basketball King and Queen and held a dance to honor them. Our senior year we were elected King and Queen, but that year neither the King nor Queen attended the dance. On that cold evening, I sat in my car out in the parking lot alone, awash in the pain of not being able to go in and enjoy the dance. The cold seat, cold dashboard, and slight frost on the windows mirrored my lonely chill in the single blue light of the gravel lot. I wept. My father didn't demand this. I thought I was honoring the teachings of our church.

I don't remember ever talking to Rheda about her experience. Many Saturday nights I drove a triangle of hot, sultry Texas towns: Rio Hondo, San Benito and Harlingen, repeatedly, alone.

On the lonely roads, I wasn't discovered or didn't have to defend not doing what others were doing: they violated the 'church things' — movies, dances. Dating helped alleviate the loneliness. For some reason I didn't want my parents to know my pain and loneliness.

I also found strength in knowing that I would attend our church's college, Bethany Nazarene College, in Oklahoma, and I would then be with kids just like me, who lived as I did. Was I ever in for a big surprise.

My first week at college I drove a carload of new friends to the car races. On the way home they wanted to stop for cigarettes and beer.

I was stunned. This was just like High School! It threw me for a loop. I didn't start smoking or drinking, but I did start questioning, "Why was I different? Was I just naïve?" Confusion, hurt and disappointment were my other new friends, and again I was alone and lonely.

I was shaken. Slowly my commitment and my strength ebbed. I began missing church and started playing cards: a definite church no-no. Honestly, it was more the hurt and isolation rather than any rebellious urge, but I was slipping. I married Shirley my sophomore year and she had long questioned 'church things'. So we knew enough to say, "No" to 'church things', but not enough to do anything else, so we drifted.

By 1966, three years out of college, I worked as an Insurance Adjustor and I averaged closing more files per month than the other adjustors. I was driven to look good and hopefully, be good. The good, moral beliefs on which I was raised had made me almost schizophrenic — dying on the inside, good on the outside.

Dying on the inside

Good on the outside showed to my regional VP who traveled up from Dallas to assess our Oklahoma City office. He talked with the other adjustors, and when he came to me he said, "Now Gary, I already know that you all need another adjustor here."

I responded, "No sir. I don't agree. I have more case files than any of the other adjustors in the office, and I still have time on my hands. What we need are more adjustors that want to work." He stared back, saying nothing.

He smiled, left and later went out with the other adjustors each night for a few drinks, but he chose none of them to take him to the airport to catch his flight back to Dallas. That surprised me, as I had not had any further contact with him after my interview.

We made small talk on the way until he said, "You know, Gary, it would do you a lot of good, help you advance in the company if you occasionally went out at night with the other guys." That hit me hard. I responded, "Now that you have helped me understand that I work for a company that bases it promotions not only on my performance at work, but my extracurricular activity as well, I need to know if I turn my resignation in to you or turn it in back at the office."

I went on to tell him that my father had pretty much always worked two and three jobs, always so I could get a college degree. I explained to him that had my father thought that getting a degree would require me to go out at night and party with the guys, that he would have preferred that I remain on the farm. Actually, I too would have preferred that.

We drove on in silence, just the sound of the air conditioner blowing. He actually began to shed tears. Time slowed. He said, "Gary, I compromised. You won't need to do that. If anyone passes you over, you call me and you have a better job in Dallas."

Again, on the outside, I was living 'church things' but I had to travel out of town. It was traveling for the company that showed me I was dying on the inside.

I had been traveling out of town for almost a year, when I entered a liquor store for the first time in my life, to buy whiskey and return to my room to drink it. I had fought the temptation, and fought it and finally given in to it.

I still hadn't smoked or uttered a curse word. I mean I didn't even repeat curse words in songs. I was as good as I knew how to be.

I returned to my room to drink. Instead, I poured all of it in the commode without taking one drink. I broke down weeping without even taking a sip. I knew I needed a Savior.

My sin drove me to the place where I knew I could not make it without a Savior. My sin was revealing me to myself. My sin presented the evidence: I could never be good enough doing 'church things'.

Finally on a Sunday afternoon I told Shirley I wanted to go to church. Life was getting out of control. I needed help. I took the family and we attended church for the first time in months. We attended a revival, and at the end of the service, I wanted to go forward, but I sensed the Lord speak to me, urging me to meet Him alone after putting the family to bed. I did. I drove out under the stars to the west of Oklahoma City, by Lake Overholser that night of February 17, 1966. I was alone in the car again like all those nights in High School, but not lonely this time.

The cold had created a slight mist on the water and the city lights glowed against the night. All the house lights being off made the night somehow darker, making me feel more alone with God, and the stars reminded me He was so large, so powerful — so present and with me.

I ached as I told God: "God please come into my life and take over."

In my home church, they didn't preach of a 'born again experience', or 'inviting God into our lives.' We preached about asking for forgiveness — a lot.

Immediately after inviting God into my life, I removed a ring, not my wedding ring, as there would be no other jewelry now, and threw it into Lake Overholser. The instant I heard the ring splash in the water, the thought went through my head, "You silly outfit, that isn't what it is all about".

That feeling — "that isn't what it is all about" — started my search. I had to find "what *it was* all about." I knew what life in Christ *wasn't*, but I didn't know what *it was*.

So I began searching to find what it was all about that God was speaking to me.

There now lived in me a power to deal with sin that I never had before. I could feel His power. I rejected many of the things against which I had struggled, without near the struggle as before.

My job moved us to Houston and there we pursued church with renewed vigor. I did everything you can do without becoming a pastor. I led music in services; we were in church, we *were there* if anyone was there. I served as the youngest man on our Church Board and President of the Houston Layman's League. I spoke in area churches. Church was our life. With our old college friends everything seemed good. Outwardly, the 'church things' were going well, but then one day I got a phone call from a beautiful lady, a friend of our family from Oklahoma.

Fran[2] was now divorced, living in Oklahoma City. She told me what I had always sensed: she had always had a thing for me. Now she wanted to come down to Houston and go with me to the beach in Galveston for a weekend. At first, it was easy. "No."

When she called again for the third time, I knew I was beginning to weaken. When I did decide to spend a weekend in Galveston with her, it "worked out" that the very weekend she would come was at the end of a week that my wife and children would be visiting my wife's family in Oklahoma.

I drove my family from Houston to Belton, Texas where we spent the weekend with my parents. On Sunday afternoon my wife and kids were riding to Muskogee with my mother. After

---

[2] Not her name.

they left, I sat down at my parents' kitchen to write my dad a letter. He was ministering at a nursing home.

Sitting in the afternoon sun, I met his absence with mixed feelings, relief, shame, and sadness. I told him what I had scheduled in Galveston, and this was so odd. I asked him to pray for me that God would intervene. I returned home to Houston alone and thankfully, God intervened. God intervened!

Knowing my family was out of town, one of my salesmen invited me to a revival that Wednesday night. I went gladly. It was the middle of a revival, a Wednesday night. The pastor stepped up to the podium to tell us that the evangelist would miss that night due to illness — the only time in over thirty years of that evangelist's ministry. That was odd.

That was only the beginning. The pastor shared that he had gone to his study that morning and became so engrossed in a Bible passage that he prepared a message to preach "someday". The evangelist called in sick and the pastor knew that "someday" was that night.

Something else strange was his message topic: sanctification. Revivals in our church followed a formula. I knew that he shouldn't preach a message on sanctification until the revival's last night, not on a Wednesday. I smiled, but inwardly I was stirred.

He began to preach. He showed us in the Bible that once God sanctifies us, sin no longer holds any power in our lives. I hung on the truth of that. *The Bible* seemed more real than his words or his sermon.

The entire room disappeared, and it was just God and I. I said, "God, if what this man is saying is true, that is what I want more than anything else." I continued focused, listening, almost nervous. I responded to his invitation at the end of the sermon. That was odd,

> **The entire room disappeared, and it was just God and I.**

too. I was the only one to respond. I felt that God had arranged this service just for me, and it made sense that I would be the only one to respond to Him, to His reaching that night.

I still had business to finish when I got home that night: alone, but not lonely.

I called and cancelled the trip to Galveston. I sat in my own personal storm of emotions and remembered to make another call.

I called my father. I told him that God had intervened. I would not be going on the trip. I choked a little to tell my hero so great and difficult a thing. He was quiet, and then he responded: "Well then, I can go eat." Suddenly, I was humbled and blown away.

There was silence. Then dad shared that he had begun praying and fasting for me after finding my note on Sunday. And my father told my Heavenly Father that he would not eat another bite until he heard from his son — that everything was all right.

For three months or so I was on a high, thinking, "This sanctification deal really worked."

Then the old challenges started coming back. My familiar doubts came with those old challenges, and I became confused, again.

I told my wife something was wrong with our church's doctrine. I said,

"Either our church doctrine is in error, or

"I don't have what it takes to live the Christian life, or

"The whole thing's a scam: a bunny rabbit and Santa Claus story."

But, I intended to find answers, and would explore the first two options first.

Arriving at the bottom of the pit.

At this time, I was a sales manager for Preferred Risk Insurance, a non-drinkers company. They promoted me from

Houston to Denver to take over the Denver sales office. It was a great step up in the company.

It was May and spring was beautiful in Houston and coming on strong in Oklahoma. As we drove to Colorado, we would drive through Oklahoma to visit Shirley's folks in Muskogee. Another spiritual storm was brewing inside me. I had a hunger that I could not name or fill. Driving through Dallas and heading north to Muskogee, my storm inside grew even as the spring sunshine brightened Shirley's and the children's spirits. We got to Muskogee.

I knew I was in no condition to go to Denver, much less to lead a sales team that needed strong leadership. I knew that I first had to resolve this spiritual issue.

So with no money to sustain my family, and after calling my Sales Manager who lived in Colorado to inform him of my decision, I unloaded our furniture in Muskogee! My wife, Shirley, was pregnant with our third child!! God only knows what I was thinking when I told the Regional Manager that I would not go to Denver. I was a young 28-year-old man with a pregnant wife and two small boys, but I knew we would make it.

Miraculously, the company offered to keep me on full salary while we decided what to do. I would not decide from May to November what God already knew!

I averaged four to six hours a day, studying the Bible and praying, "God, I don't care where it takes me, or what it does to me. Just show me truth, something that will work in my life!"

Occasionally I woke up my pregnant wife to show her what I was finding. I can't imagine how hard that was for her. She had a husband who

> *I give them eternal life, and they shall never perish; no one can snatch them out of my hand. My Father, who has given them to me, is greater than all; no one can snatch them out of my Father's hand.*
> John 10:28-29

didn't know what to tell his employer about work, but he was waking her in the middle of the nights excitedly asking, "Can you believe this? After what we were taught, can you believe the Bible says this?" I laugh looking back, but I loved those days. God was using His Word, His evidence to show me that He was Truth.

I searched the scriptures for hours day after day, and those hours passed like minutes. I loved searching the evidence of who the Bible said Jesus was, rather than listening to other men tell me who they thought He was. I finally understood some important parts of my father and his passion for the Word.

It is hard to describe those days. I awoke in the nights and first thing in the mornings, hungry to read. All the wonderful things I read and learned the previous day crowded out my sleep, and I could only think — "I wonder what I will find tomorrow?"

> "Present your case," says the LORD. "Set forth your arguments." Isaiah 41: 21-22.
>
> "Review the past for Me, let us argue the matter together. State the case for your innocence." Isaiah 43:26

Repeatedly, I found that my answers for life weren't sufficient for Life as it came at me. God let me "build my case" using my thoughts, traditions, and what I thought I knew without testing it, and then He would blow gently on all of it. His breath vaporized my sham sentiments, and obliterated 'things that never were Truth.'

In place of all of that 'nothing,' God presented His case, His evidence in the Bible as I hungrily thumbed the pages of what was becoming *His Word to me*!

I started seeing what theologians call eternal security — something I had heard preached against all my life in my church. Eternal security says that if we surrender our all to God in Christ, that we can rest there: confident in what Christ did for us. We rest because we are more confident in what Christ did *for* us and *in* us than all we'll ever do. Here we experience God's salvation, or we're born again as some say.

The Bible's evidence made me fearful. You see, as far as I was concerned, the only reality keeping me out of trouble was that I did not want to go to hell when I died. Very strong in our 'church things' was a belief that where we go at the end of life depends on what we are doing at the time of death. If I was being obedient and good when I died, then I went to heaven. If I died at a bad time in my life, then God's eternal verdict for me was bad. Eternity depended on the timing of my death, which robbed me of any peace. My motivator to do good was if I died "bad' or "away from God' then all bets were off. I would be lost.

Now, in those hot summer weeks, in those hours in the Word, by the lake, when I finally gave in to the evidence, and saw in His Word for myself that I was eternally saved — then what love filled my heart and flooded my being! I moved from thinking that everything depended on me for saving, and trusted that God had done His unshakable work. His Word, His love, His evidence to me, to all of His children was clear to me. All the 'saving' really lay with God. More than all I did in my life, what God did for me secured me to Him forever as His child. I enjoyed a secure feeling I had never known.

My motivation shifted. God's love now coursed more powerfully through me than the fear that had motivated me for so many years. Wow, what a difference.

As I had searched for Truth all those hours every day — studying, praying, occasionally staying at home on Friday nights instead of going to ball games with my family — I burned; I yearned to find His Truth to satisfy and sustain me in my walk. I thirsted for Him.

God was letting me make my feeble cases for life, and then overwhelming me with His evidence.

Only recently did I realize how God walked a 28-year-old 'kid' away from teachings that his family, his professors, and his friends all held, saying to them, "It's wrong. What you know, and teach is not Truth." Only now do I see the enormity of my shift. I was not only rejecting the teaching of my youth, but those that had taught me as well.

And I realize now that this first step to trust a God, who wanted me to be eternally secure was only the first phase of a revolution He was fomenting in me.

Something else God did: He changed my evidentiary basis. That's lawyerese for "what is the most unshakable sort of evidence" on which to base my case? My evidence for Christianity had been preachers and friends. It had included traditions, those 'church things' that my wife and I had begun rejecting back in college. Now, for the first time in my life the basis, the only unshakable evidence was the Bible, the scriptures, or my favorite term for them: the Word or God's Word.

However, Preferred Risk was getting anxious over my six months in Muskogee with no decision as to where I would be with the company. By the end of six months I had turned down the company's offer to move to three or four different cities as a Sales Manager.

When I came to a peace about being secure in my relationship to God, my life's immovable areas began to move. God now presented the evidence of His plan, His truth at work, not only on the Bible's pages, but also now in my life.

First, as cool weather arrived in Oklahoma and the trees began to turn, Shirley and our boys walked with me into First Baptist Church to join. My first time to ever attend a Baptist service, we joined.

Second, I addressed my problem with my 'old church'. The pastor there wanted me to come and speak. I repeatedly declined, but after his continual insistence, I finally agreed to speak on a Sunday night.

I rose to speak, not knowing how the night would go. I spoke on the very first verse in the Psalms. I poured out what had happened to me. I pointed out that they all knew me and knew my parents, and that we all knew many who were missing from the service — their children.

> Blessed is the man who does not walk in the counsel of the ungodly — Psalm 1:1

I pointed to empty pews that their kids had left empty that morning, and the previous week, month and year before. Their children might come out of respect for their parents on Easter, Christmas, and Mother's Day, but they were missing.

I asked, "Why isn't this faith which is so important to you, important to your kids?"

I said, "I can't speak for them, but I can speak for myself and tell you that if it wasn't for the Grace of God in my life, I wouldn't be in church tonight either."

"Why?"

I paused because this was hard to know and harder to say.

"You taught your kids, as my parents taught me —things that never were Truth. You gave us long lists of "don'ts." You warned us not to own TVs, eat out on Sundays, and never to wear jewelry, because if we did, we would cease being a Christian." I listed more things, stopped, looked up and said, "I can see from the looks on your faces that your thinking, 'Oh, Gary, but we've quit keeping those lists!'"

I took in a breath to say, "Really?"

"You may say you no longer keep lists, but how about smoking and drinking? Are you saying those aren't on your list?" I assured them that I knew they were. They had only shrunk their list of things that kept someone out of Heaven.

No one moved. I went on to explain, "I have found One, who is sufficient in my life!"

"And the lists never were Truth. Your lists without God's assurance and love have emptied this place."

I continued, "I have found what — no, I have found Who is more sustaining than your list, and that is a born again relationship with Christ. My sustainer."

It was so quiet. No one moved. No one coughed. No one looked away. I suggested that they test the 'real thing' — Christ — by whether or not their children would start to return. I closed saying, "If you were my parent and you asked my forgiveness for having taught me things as truth that weren't truth, I might be back here Sunday."

I finished and waited to be stoned. People did press in on me, but they wanted to talk to me, and asked, "Why don't you go into the ministry, Gary?" Four couples visited our home asking me to speak with their children. I gently told them they needed to do that themselves, and ask their children to forgive them. As I said, I addressed my problem with our old church.

Third, I was learning something new about life — how God works His plan in us. Not only did God work it, He told me what He would do ahead of time, a rare experience and something entirely new to me.

Again, God continued presenting His evidence for a beautiful plan in my life!

What God told me seemed impossible.

I would return to Houston on January first.

I would return to be the company's Houston Sales Manager: the job I had left to be transferred to Colorado. That job in Houston had been filled. I knew it was where I would be. How could I *know*? God spoke to me. He made it known to me. However you say that, I had a *knowing*.

I would re-enroll in law school: something akin to skiing up Everest.

When I called my Regional Manager the week before Thanksgiving to tell him I knew I would be back in Houston on

January 1, Mr. Bolander assured me that my replacement was doing a good job, that no change was needed, that he could see no way a change could be made. I told him not to worry, it would simply happen. I couldn't explain it so that he would understand, and in response to his question, no, I hadn't talked to Ben, the man who had replaced me.

The day after Thanksgiving, Mr. Bolander called to say Ben's resignation letter was lying on his desk when he came in to work that morning. I should load up and report back to Houston. I did and later when I asked permission to re-enroll in Law School, the company said, "No." I enrolled for summer school, nonetheless, and in the process of enrolling the lady said, "You are a very lucky man, but I guess you know that!"

I told her, "Yes, I do feel that way," but I explained that I had no idea why she thought I was lucky. I had no idea what she was trying to tell me.

So she explained, "If you had waited until the fall to register, you would have lost all 32 hours of your work, which I see is almost straight A's. You would have had to completely start Law School over!"

I stood there blinking.

There it was again. God was presenting evidence to me, like He does to you. God was doing His work in my life: leading, guiding, and completing me.

I was experiencing more of God's evidence in my life. He was my Protector.

In law school I fell in love with trial law. I loved amassing evidence, and particularly loved strategizing how to present the evidence to a jury, to put Truth on trial and let it speak for itself. God at the same time was presenting His case for Himself to Gary Richardson.

When my manager returned to Houston, I told him that I had registered for law school and that I would understand it if he terminated me.

He said, "I never want to discuss it again." End of story: and more evidence that God was presenting to me: God was my Protector. He showed His evidence: first in the Bible, and now again in my life.

God did such an astounding job of presenting His case on this first point, that once I was His I could rest in that — I had to know more of Him. And search I did.

And not once, never since I came to believe in my eternal security in God, have I ever wavered from this belief, even during my eleven years in the wilderness, which ended ten years ago, never did I question where I would go at death. What a peace, but God was making a case and presenting it to me, and He had only begun.

Again, I began to search for God, or His Truth, His plan for me for us. I would have loved for that search to lead me to great libraries, to astounding seminaries, and wise teachers.

My 'teachers' were to be of a very different sort.

2

UNLEARNING AND LETTING GO

Behold, [Jesus] is coming with clouds. —Revelation 1:7 In the Bible clouds are always associated with God. Clouds are the sorrows, sufferings, or providential circumstances, within or without our personal lives, which actually seem to contradict God's sovereignty. Yet through these very clouds God's Spirit is teaching us how to walk by faith.

It is not true to say that God wants to teach us something in our trials. Through every cloud He brings our way, He wants us to *unlearn* something. His purpose in using the cloud is to simplify our beliefs until our relationship with Him is exactly like that of a child.

— *My Utmost for His Highest*, Oswald Chambers July 29.

As God presented me the Biblical evidence of who He was, who He really was, I loved learning Truth. I drank it in. I drank Him in. I was already hungry for more truth about God, such as His holding me securely forever once I belonged to Him.

But something came easily for me that did not come easily for others, nor would it always come easily for me. For God to form Truth in us, traditions, half-truths, and outright lies must be let go. They must be *unlearned*.

Because I was so hungry for His love, so starved for His security, dropping my old teaching was a no-brainer. Leaving behind what "never was truth" took no energy. As God opened my eyes, old

> *"Your traditions say...*
> *but I tell you."*
> —Jesus

teachings began to leave. I told them to pack their baggage out with them. I did not miss them. Four decades later, I have yet to mourn them.

Yet I had not yet understood why Jesus launched His ministry by telling people: "*Repent*, for the kingdom of heaven is at hand.[3]"

Now repent means that I am doing 75 mph down the turnpike, realize that my GPS says I am headed the wrong way, and I swerve through four lanes to exit, go under the overpass, and hop back on the turnpike headed the other way as fast as I can.

'Repent' means doing a 180°. More than changing direction, merging to the right or curving to the left, it's a complete reversal. Christians nod and say, "Yes, that's 'repentance'." And they are right, but they are thinking of obvious wrong directions like having an affair, doing drugs, or embezzling money from your boss.

Jesus found that the people who least wanted to repent were religious folks. They had gotten things 'right', so they thought, and were now terribly invested in their beliefs — whether or not those beliefs were true, truly biblical, or true pictures of God.

Unlearning

Oswald Chambers gives us my favorite way of phrasing this repenting from religious or 'church things': *unlearning*. We must unlearn the beliefs that are pushing us away from God, to learn what will take us the right way — closer to God — more into His image.

As I said, I loved pouring over the Bible for hours a day, and waking up my wife in the night to share the "WOW" things I was finding.

In the last chapter I not only loved what I was learning, I loved *the way* I was learning. In this chapter I want to be honest

---

[3] Matthew 4:17 (NASB)

about two hard ways we must learn in life: unlearning and letting go.

As an athlete, I easily took so many things for granted, as my birthright: balance, speed, quickness, and eyesight. I took my eyesight for granted playing tennis and basketball, working, and playing with my children.

So I had no reason to fear going to the optometrist that day in 1969.

Everything was routine: the clean smells of the doctor's office, dilating my eyes, his clean, crisp white coat. I breezed through the eye chart, and he then turned out the lights and took the little, bright white light and peered into my eyes as I stared where he told me. As always, he examined the right eye quickly, and he then began examining my left eye.

The optometrist held his breath while he was in my face. After a while, I was holding my breath as well.

He sat back on his stool and asked, "How did you injure your left eye?"

My mind raced. I replied, "I don't remember. I don't remember injuring my eye."

He was quiet. So quiet. He resumed looking into my left eye.

Then he talked, using big terms, but in English he finally said he wanted to send me to a specialist as he thought my left eye had been injured and he thought I was losing that eye. I went numb inside. What do you say? How do you react to losing an eye? Being young, ambitious, athletic and a winner couldn't help. I was devastated.

I went to his specialist who confirmed his concern and concurred. I would lose the eye.

I drove home. After hearing the specialist's diagnosis I was shaken. Both doctors said the same thing. I would lose the eye and suddenly all the little things about which I might have complained — the hot car, dry weather, financial challenges — they all seemed like nothing. I was losing an eye.

Now I was quiet, finally I was quiet inside — quiet enough to unlearn.

I wanted to trust God with losing my eye, because nothing else could help or made sense. I had not arrived at what to say, or how to trust God with this. I did not know it at the time, but I was unlearning.

I could not hold on to my eye, or make it work. How could I be 'in charge' of my life when I could not even keep my eyes working?

My thoughts and prayers came fuzzily.

I never did pray for healing. I prayed only for His will to be done, knowing that His will is always best — even if that meant losing my eye. I could trust Him. I was unlearning. You see, down deep I had believed that 'God's best' for me included the best body and intelligence, the best marriage, and maybe the best clothes and cars.

But I was going to lose an eye. And with losing that eye, I would lose a cherished assumption: because God loved me, my body would always be healthy. Wrong. Unlearned. Not if God wanted to do something in me that necessitated losing the eye. I then had to learn something new: God could easily have another plan for me, for my body, for my growth.

> *Endure hardship as discipline; God is treating you as sons. For what son is not disciplined by his father? If you are not disciplined (and everyone is), then you are illegitimate children and not true sons.*
> Hebrews 12:7-8

And that was that. I accepted losing my eye if that was part of God's plan for my life. I was unlearning. I was unlearning that I was in control of my life. I could not add a breath to the length of my life, and neither I, nor any doctor could save my eye.

Soon afterward, we moved back to Houston. For three years I awoke every day, half expecting to have lost the left eye, trusting

God and denying the reality — all at the same time! In '72 I went to have my eyes checked again. All I got was confirmation. A Houston optometrist sent me to his specialist. Both confirmed I would lose my left eye.

I had to unlearn and say what I trusted; finally say what I had unlearned.

I had wanted to be on a straightaway, following God, but I felt like I was living in a cul-de-sac and taking laps on the same lesson — trusting God, denial, not sure exactly how to pray! So on the way home that day I said out loud in the car, "God, I don't know how my losing my eye could bring you glory, but I do know that unless it was bringing You glory, I would not be losing the eye, and I accept that."

At age thirty I gained as much confidence in God's hand as I had ever had in anything. For years I wore glasses, taking it for granted a time would come when I would wake up and my left eye would be dark. I went for a check-up in '89, because my lens prescription no longer seemed to work. I thought I needed a stronger prescription.

It was eerie. The ophthalmologist cheerily read my chart, checked my vision, and got quiet. He turned off the lights and pulled out that little light. He peered into my left eye. Quiet. Finally, he left and returned with all my records.

> No discipline seems pleasant at the time, but painful. Later on, however, it produces a harvest of righteousness and peace for those who have been trained by it. Hebrews 12:11

My heart sank. Was this the time to lose my eye? I was curiously at peace. I had unlearned and learned trust about my eyes years ago. The doctor returned to show me my readings over the years on my left eye. He confirmed to me (and himself!) that I had needed glasses for almost twenty years, but that now, for some reason, my left eye was reading 20/20.

I haven't needed glasses since, and that was 18 years ago. I did not lose my left eye; in fact, my left eye today remains 20/20.

I did have to undergo corrective surgery, but it was on my *right* eye!

I never seriously welcomed tribulation, but then again, at times I have said, "God, if I need more tribulation in my life for You to do the work You want to do in me, I am willing."

When I remember the times when I say those words, I am contrite. We don't look forward to tribulation, but we do look for the growth that comes out of it — unlearning gets us to that point.

At other times in my life, when things were really tough, I've said, "God, this I do know, that the tougher times get, the greater the miracle, and I totally trust You with my life and my circumstances."

During those times, when I grew in knowledge, *I was unlearning as fast as I was learning.* So much has to be "unlearned" in order for us to "learn" who God is in our lives and how He works.

Not that all that I believe is truth *is in fact* truth! I am sure I have blindness that God will show me as time passes! Blindness comes from pride, which is the opposite of how He takes us anywhere — in humility. Unlearning is about dumping our pride in any cherished belief, any notion that keeps us from seeing the truer, bigger picture of God and His plan for us.

Unlearning applies to so many areas of our lives. I know women whose marital challenges come from 'unmanning' their husbands. My point to my friend, Elana, was that until she quit doing things that her husband should be doing, until she pulled back, that she would never have a good marriage to a man; to a "wimp", sure, but not to the man who was my friend.

I said, "Your husband will not wrestle with you for control."

She responded, "But what happens if Brett doesn't do the things that must be done? What happens if I don't step in and do them?"

I answered, "You go down together."

You could see it in her face: terror. Brett was Elana's third husband, and her two prior husbands had both cheated on her.

I gently said, "Elana, God's Word calls you to be Brett's 'helper'.[4] It calls you to trust Brett as though trusting God through him.[5] Elana, when you take the lead, you are telling God, 'I can't trust You, or Your plan for my marriage, because Brett will fail me *here* and *there*.' When you quit taking the lead, Brett will pick it up. He will fulfill his role before the ship goes down completely. You do what God has said for you to do as his wife, and trust God with it."

Her fear still held her, but she heard the truth. She had to let go of the control that was stealing her husband's manhood. She had to unlearn marriage as she had known it, and I have watched Elana make major changes in herself, and in her relationship to Brett — with amazing results.

She was unlearning a role that had not worked twice already while she simultaneously learned to trust God with her marriage, even her very personality. In humility, she unlearned and trusted God for a marriage she had never experienced, and saw changes in Brett.

Elana was unlearning-to-learn that healthy leaders partner (both in business and in marriage) to reach their goals. Paul reminds us[6] that nothing endangers leaders more than unhealthy or destructive partnerships. See some signs of good partnerships:
1. The parties share the same values.
2. The parties agree on the goal(s).
3. No parties compromise their convictions, especially if they are based on solid Biblical understanding.
4. No party selfishly demands that the other surrender.
5. No party benefits while the other loses.

---

[4] Genesis 2:18, 20 and following.
[5] Ephesians 5:22
[6] 2 Cor 6:14-18

Good partnerships do not foster codepenence or independence, but *interdependence*. Each party feels secure, is stretched, and enjoys the synergy. The partnership multiplies the productivity of both parties.

What irreducible, unmistakable, absolute has to be in me to unlearn and learn at a tough time in my life? Humility —
>Humility is perpetual quietness of thought.
>It is to have no trouble.
>It is never to be fretted, vexed, irritable or sore.
>to wonder at nothing that is done to me;
>and to fret nothing done against me.
>It is to be at rest when nobody praises me. . .
>and when I am blamed or despised.
>It is to have a blessed home within myself...
>where I can go in and shut the door...
>and kneel to my Father in secret.
>Humility is to be at peace as a deep sea of calmness...
>when around and about me is trouble.

Humility has become my secret "weapon" during seasons of testing, when clouds gather and storms swirl around me. When fear instead of faith, or fear instead of peace, or fear instead of calm besets me, it is time to become humble — again.

Letting Go

I have had ample places to be humble.

Take forgiveness. I have had to learn to give and receive it, and nothing teaches us about humbly letting go more than forgiveness.

Years ago, my wife's close friend and business associate came to complain to me about her. I stopped her. There was nothing about Sandy that she would tell me that I already didn't know, and I cautioned her that she would feel badly later for having said it. She was still charged and serious.

I told her that if later she still needed to vent, to call and she could vent. Three days later she called and vented. Sandy's and my marriage was in a rocky place, and I prayed that maybe hearing these things from a friend in my presence would make an impact. I asked, "Would you sit down and say to Sandy what you said to me?"

She replied, "No. It would destroy our friendship and working relationship."

I asked, "Which is more important: reaching Sandy, or your friendship?"

Days later Sandy and I were talking when Mary Ann called. I asked in Sandy's presence, "Would you be willing to come over and have the discussion you had with me?"

She agreed to do so, and came over.

Once she was in my wife's presence, though, she completely whitewashed all she had said to me, immediately making Sandy's situation and mine even worse. I felt betrayed, and the odd man out. I knew my marriage was worse off, and she hurt me.

I struggled with releasing that friend, forgiving her for so long. Then I unlearned what I knew of forgiveness and came to the "letting go" time. Regardless of what someone has done to harm us, the process of being able to come to a place of forgiveness and letting it go, is always the same.

That process focuses on God — on Him as my Protector — so that no one can harm me without God's allowing it, and when He does, He is allowing it (sometimes causing it) for one reason: God is doing a work in

> Don't become
> so well adjusted
> to your culture
> that you fit into it
> without even thinking.
> Instead,
> fix your attention on God.
> You'll be changed
> from the inside out.
> Readily recognize
> what He wants from you,
> and quickly respond to it.
> Unlike the culture around you,
> always dragging you down
> to its level of immaturity,
> God brings the best out of you,
> develops well-formed maturity
> in you.
> Romans 12:2

me. God is allowing / causing it to make me more into His image.

When I really see that, when I really believe it; it is a WOW moment.

My friends all expect to hear that now, "WOW." A WOW comes when I see God's hand, His purpose revealed. It hits me that God's sovereign plan was really, really good. It washes through me that God's will for my life in this or that situation is far beyond what I could have imagined or engineered or manipulated if I had gotten everything I wanted.

So again, when I focus on God as my protector or provider, I stay in forgiveness by renewing my mind as often as I must, until I know it has been forgiven and released.

What then is the basis of unlearning, of letting go? The same basis as leaves letting go of trees every fall.

Fall in Colorado renews me. I love the gold of Aspen groves, the blue-green of the forests, and the colder air with whispers of snow. In the fall of 2000, I heard a man say that, *"everything in our lives is a gift."*

I literally bristled at hearing that. I didn't believe it to be true and I certainly knew there were many things going on in my life that I would not describe as *gifts* — how could they be? Also, the speaker wasn't even a preacher; he was a lawyer, and as far as I

> Every desirable and beneficial gift comes out of heaven. The gifts are rivers of light cascading down from the Father of Light. There is nothing deceitful in God, nothing two-faced, nothing fickle.
> James 1:17

know, not even a person that professed to be a Christian. But, seven years later, after the seed was planted in me in that bright fall of 2000, I can truthfully say that I see everything that comes into my life today as something that God will use as a gift — everything — especially the things that were hard to forgive, to unlearn, or to let go.

I had to forgive a private investigator and personal friend who promised to wreck my life over a money matter that I had entrusted to my partners while I campaigned for governor. I returned six months later to find they had not done as I had promised my friend. Too late. He had resigned and I wasn't told what happened. My partners said he would destroy me, which surprised me until I learned that they hadn't bonused him as I promised. Then I understood his anger. My wife, now ex-wife, testified under oath that my friend had called and told her things damaging to our marriage that I knew were untrue. I even offered to take a polygraph test over the things my ex-wife claimed he called to tell her.

To have any peace, I had to find the same place where I had rested when specialists confirmed I would lose my eye, and did. It took weeks, but I regularly renewed my mind to be able to forgive my former investigator. Happily, today our friendship is restored and we both benefit from it again. *Question*: Is this not a better way to live our lives than to nurse old grudges that both destroy our once beautiful relationships and also keep us from having that perfect peace with Jesus? I find renewing my mind to be better. I trust that you will as well. I was able to test this again.

I thought my friend and long time financial partner, Jim,[7] made a series of bad business moves, and it appeared to me that he had attempted to cover them as things worsened. I was devastated to "learn" what he was doing. We had scheduled golf a couple of days later. We both showed and played. I had asked Jim to provide me the amount of the money that I thought he should have paid into our projects and knew he was working on it. I never mentioned it: neither did Jim.

I knew I must get over my pain, not give in to anger, and reach a place of forgiveness before I could address the matter.

My worldly pride told me he *owed* me. I had to forgive Jim or lose a valued friend. I couldn't let money be the issue, nor

---

[7] Not his real name.

could my pride dictate my actions. This was enough of a starting place.

I worked through my pain for four days, working at letting it go, repeatedly turning loose of all my pride's *stuff*. For four days I renewed my mind with Scriptures on forgiveness and reminded myself that nothing could happen to me unless God either brought it or allowed it. I worked through my pain and impulse to anger. I was ready to hear from my friend, hear his story. Finally I could *hear* Jim as he shared his story. Had I not already forgiven my friend, *before our meeting*, I would never have heard or understood him. I could not have remained in a friendship and business relationship that we had enjoyed for years.

> *Many of His disciples heard [Jesus teach] and said, 'This is tough teaching, too tough to swallow."* John 6:60
>
> *After this a lot of His disciples left. They no longer wanted to be associated with him.* John 6:66

As I listened to Jim's explanation, the situation wasn't close to what I had first thought it to be. Even so, had I not *let go* and forgiven him, I could not have heard his story. How many relationships are destroyed because we didn't reach forgiveness that enabled us to hear, really listen to the other person's story?

Again, God had shown me that unless I renew my mind time and time and time again, the pain will turn to anger. Could that be what the scripture is talking about on how many times to forgive someone? Even when I am traveling down the straightaway with God, and not stuck in some faithless cul-de-sac, I may have to 'let go' of old stuff repeatedly.

Forgiveness is for us. It is God's instructions to us. Just like seed sowing is a concept, that can be and often is distorted. So, forgiveness is something God tells us to do often. "Let it go 70 times 7 times in a day!"[8] The number isn't great when we reach a place of real forgiveness.

---

[8] Matthew 18:22

When we get there, letting go with God, then it strengthens so many other areas of our lives: family, marriage — even business.

I remember an employee, Cory, saying, "So Gary, you're practicing law again." I was a little surprised at his comment, but I had no clue as to why he would say that.

I responded, "I've been here all along, everyday as a matter of fact, unless I was out of town." But Cory was referring to my not exercising *control* in the office, and what he and others perceived as a corresponding lack of interest.

His revelation amazed me, as my interest had always been intense.

As I explored the idea with Cory I could see that for three years I had been doing exactly what I had told Elana. I was unlearning control, and learning God's uses of others in my life and business.

You see, I turned over day-to-day operations of the law firm to my son three years ago and for the first two years I continually had to restrain myself (retrain myself) from taking back control.

On taking the reins, he did and didn't do many things I would have done differently and of course, considered to have been better for the firm — maybe so, maybe no — just different styles when seen from a clear perspective.

Cory and others in the office had read my lack of "leading" as my lack of concern or interest, but I made it clear that I had turned over the running of the firm, and I would not take it back. I was simply there to help. Did I bite my tongue? Yes. Did others talk to me about it? Yes. They were nervous as my son's leadership style is so different from mine, and they were unlearning my style to learn his.

But if our firm were to have any hope for the future, if it were to pass to the next generation, then I repeatedly had to let go, and 'handle it' — by not handling it, and letting my son, the man, grow into the job.

Cory blinked, smiled, and said, "Boy, that sure answers a lot of questions for me."

He told me how the employees discussed my disengagement and wondered why I didn't appear to care or be involved. He agreed, however, if I had done as he and the other employees thought I should, that it would have most likely destroyed my relationship with my son, and very likely have destroyed the law firm.

If I trust God, I can only trust my son, and his way of leading, regardless of what happens with the law firm that I entrusted to God. We have to let go of our ideas of how things should run, succeed, and so on and trust that God has a plan and that we can trust Him. Thankfully, our firm is once again flourishing, conforming to my son's leadership style and confirming yet again — there is more than one way to do things.

Think of a minister who gloats when a church he left does not do as well with him gone. What should he have *let go* and *unlearned* before leaving so that this church would have enjoyed strengthened leaders to lead it forward when he parted?

Think of all the marriages that will only go forward if the couples both unlearn what they have been doing and let go of past hurts and failures.

How many of us are missing God's plan for our lives because we don't unlearn, and we don't let go? When we don't unlearn and let go, we want to go back and do parts of our lives over again, knowing we will do them better. Not so.

HERE ARE some other verses that help me grasp the *Unlearning* and *Letting It Go* principles

You want something but don't get it. You kill and covet, but you cannot have what you want. You quarrel and fight. You do not have, because you do not ask God. When you ask, you do not receive; because you ask with wrong motives, that you may spend what you get on your pleasures.[9]

Your Father knows what you need before you ask Him.[10]

And this is the will of Him who sent Me, that I shall lose none of all that he has given me, but raise them up at the last day.[11]

[God] who did not spare His own Son, but gave Him up for us all — how will He [God the Father] not also, along with Him [Jesus], graciously give us all things?[12]

Recently a friend said as it began to sprinkle, "I am going to pray that it won't rain." Immediately I thought and responded "Great! So if it does rain, you'll be prayed up to handle whatever God's plan is!" We both smiled. Thinking on it later, I realized that this is true in everything for which we pray. Then I thought, "Wow. What would it be like if God answered all my prayers the way I ask Him to answer them?" That would pretty much put me in control of my life. How scary would that be?

I want to add that until we are ready, really ready, to lay things down and let God raise up what He wants in our lives, we are not ready to trust Him with our lives.

But God has put in all of us a desire to see, to feel, to understand life. We phrase what we are hunting in a thousand different ways, but what we are hunting ultimately is the One who created us, who placed in us a desire to know Him. He is working in you to bring you to that place.

---

[9] James 4:2-3
[10] Matthew 6:8
[11] John 6:39
[12] Romans 8:32

3

Why Live in Regret or Shame? Enter *The Dance* With Him!

God is more sovereign than we have imagined. Picture this sign of His power.

It is a river.

Have you ever watched a powerful river coursing into the ocean? The Mississippi measures a mile across at its mouth. When Hurricane Katrina swelled its banks, it flooded, inundated, and almost exterminated New Orleans. That's power, but it's not as powerful as this river I want you to see.

According to the maps, the Amazon spans ten miles at its mouth. As they sail South America's coast, ship captains new to the area often get pushed silently off course to find themselves unwittingly far out in the Atlantic as they sail through the mighty Amazon's emptying itself. That's powerful, but nothing in comparison to this river. This river is quieter, immutable, unstoppable.

Up and down the Mississippi and the Amazon, ships, tugs and barges ply with their cargos, but no one has ever sailed, swam, or powered upriver an inch in this river.

People swim the mouths of the Mississippi and the Amazon. You can swim from side to side in God's power river and Einstein theorized you could swim downstream, but no one has that we know.

The amazing thing about this river is that you can't see it, but you can't miss its effects. Everything it washes — it washes away, or wears down, or wears out. And it washes *everything* you see.

We do keep track of its current — always. We wear 'current markers' on our wrists. We flip open our phones and read current markers for this river. Our computers, DVD players, stoves, coffee makers, and cars all sport current markers. These current markers of which I am speaking are called timepieces — watches.

The river of which I am speaking is *time*.

None of us will ever escape this river. We can swim sideways in the river of time all we want, traveling all over the globe if we wish.

Maybe someone will swim downstream at unimaginable expense by traveling in space and returning to earth, or so theorized Einstein. Yet we know this: no one has ever swum upstream, except for men named Hezekiah and Joshua, and they were on little excursions with God.

No one has ever returned to a point upstream, or back in time to change a moment in his or her life — no matter how much we all wish we could.

God, and God alone, travels outside this river of time, and He alone makes it possible for anyone else to live outside of time.

Time is a mark of God's sovereignty, and we wrestle within it all of our lives. It is not so bad until at some point downstream we receive new insights. When we get these insights about an event upriver, back in time we tend to beat ourselves up for what we did in the past that we now see better. We see that we weren't smart or Godly. We use our newly learned insights, possibly gleaned from the very event that now shames us to condemn ourselves, which may not be enough. We also see ourselves wrong and wreak havoc in our present lives. We react similarly if we find something terribly human or failed about Christian brothers and sisters. We beat up on them as if they should have been perfect.

My favorite devotional writer for a few years has been Oswald Chambers. I have given his devotional books to friends and family and have enjoyed his writings daily. Chambers says this about our 'new insights',[13] "If the Spirit of God detects anything in you that is wrong, He does not ask you to put it right; He asks you to accept [His] light on it, and He will put it right." This is one of God's normal, healthy methods of growing us.

What is it like to you as a believer, when God "asks you to accept His light on" something He is showing you about your past?

"God's Light" outed Ted

Colorado pastor, Ted Haggard, sinned. Pastor of a large Colorado church, he headed an evangelical organization for North America. He seemingly had a devoted family, Christian friends and yes, something in his life that God wanted to expose.

He sinned. It became public, but ugly as it seemed, in God's time, it will be seen by us as beautiful. God did not expose Ted's sin just to bring pain to him, to his family, and to his church, but to usher Ted into a place where God would do a work in his life. Our loving God had a plan for Ted's life. Still does. God was working in Ted Haggard's life just as He is in our lives.

God never leaves us, or leaves us alone by forsaking us. He can't. It is not in His nature.

See it from God's wisdom, from His point of view. Even in all that Haggard has endured God is at work, and when God is working (He *always* is!), it is beautiful. Pastor Haggard reached a point where God needed to do a new work in him. All of us, like Ted, have work that needs finishing in us. Now I am convinced, the more vocal we are about our goodness or perceived perfection, the more public our light and sin.

---

[13] Chambers, Oswald. (1935). March 23 in *My Utmost for His Highest: Selections for the Year*, McClelland and Stewart Limited, Toronto.

Ted sheltered a dark secret in hotel rooms with other men, so we have been told. Simply stated: that secret part of Ted's life was no secret to God and not as Christ-like as God wanted it to be. We all face those times in our lives, though hopefully, not as public or as humiliating as Ted's. But they will be growing experiences, just as his will be.

Ted knew his deep secret, just as we all know our own. How much light did Ted's loving Father shine on that part of his life? Should He have stunned Ted with such a glaring light? Did the light have to be as glaring as the deception Ted paraded? Should we judge how God chooses to do His promised work in each of us?

The light turned on Ted when a man from a hotel room outed him. Ted could not or would not do it himself. Too often, neither can we nor will we. Like us, Ted ran from the light's glaring pain, its pain of change and growth.

What Ted lived in secret, even paying the man money to keep quiet, suddenly glared in the light of hundreds of newspapers, magazines, and TV talk shows. Did Ted accept the light? No. Ted first tried to cover the light that God, in His mercy, shone on his secret. Ted sinned, bringing devastation to his life, temporarily. God will use that as well, for Ted's good, just as He promised.

God led Ted to a place where he would be tempted. Jesus warned us of those places in His Model Prayer — *and lead us not into temptation, but deliver us from evil.*[14]

Satan, created to serve as tempter, was there just as God ordained. Satan tempted Ted in an area needing God's growing touch, but God directs the steps of the righteous.[15] He directed Ted's steps, knowing Ted would fall to Satan's temptation repeatedly, unless we believe this was his first time in such a

---

[14] Matthew 6:13
[15] Psalm 37:23; Psalm 119:5; Psalm 119:33, Jeremiah 10:23

room. Why would a grace-filled God allow this, even possibly purpose this to happen? God is doing what He promised all of His children. He is working in us, making us more like Him. God uses Satan to show us our need of Him. God uses Satan to show us our ugliness where God will next work in us. How can it be more beautiful? It is God's way and His sometimes-inscrutable plan for us.

Ted sinned just as a gracious God allowed or directed. Why? We don't know and never will. Thankfully, we need not know as we grow to trust Him with our lives.

Now, does this sound somewhat like Adam and Eve?

Exactly.

God let Pastor Haggard have this experience (just like all of us!) so God could continue a work in his life. God promised to continue His work relentlessly from Ted's first day of salvation until he stands before God. Paul said, "There has never been the slightest doubt in my mind that the God who started this great work in you would keep at it and bring it to a flourishing finish on the very day Christ Jesus appears."[16]

God could have prevented the entire thing from happening in many ways: a flat tire on Ted's way to the hotel, an emergency phone call, but He didn't. Why?

One reason and one reason only: God would not avert a work needing to be done in Pastor Haggard's life.

You might argue with God that there were surely some better ways for God to have done this work and kept it under wraps. You might raise the question, "But what of Ted's reputation, his image?"

Let me ask you this. "Do you think God is more interested in Ted's image or in Ted's growth as His child? Is God One to cover up our sin, or assist us in covering it? Or is God at work in us to make us more like Him?

---

[16] Philippians 1:6 (MSG)

The answer is easy. Jesus even said, "Better to go into heaven missing an eye or arm, than to fail God doing His work in you." [17]

Then you might ask, "But what about the church that Haggard pastored?" And I respond, "Do you think God didn't see this happening?" Further, "You think God couldn't have prevented Haggard from becoming pastor there?" Of course He could have prevented it, but in His wisdom, God is doing a work in each of His children. He is more committed to that work of completing us than He will ever be in helping us keep our dark secrets, or maintaining our image in the eyes of others.

Like me, maybe you need to put down your precious image and prized reputation and beg God to do His work in you as His child. He is about His promises with or without our permission. Actually, we gave Him permission the day He re-birthed us and we must continually thank Him for never neglecting His daily work in us.

Again, what God is doing in Ted is a *beautiful* thing! God refused to help Ted hide his secret.[18]

God had in His plan a time to do a work in Ted's life. He promised to continue that new work. God keeps that promise in all of our lives after our new birth in Him. His work in us serves as a constant reminder: we need Him.

Do we see something similar in the Bible?

Paul was outed from being a Pharisee

Look at Paul's life. Do you know it? Paul was a Pharisee: super-religious.[19] God shone His light on Paul's life as he headed into the city of Damascus and soon enough, Paul counted all that

---

[17] Matthew 5:28
[18] Luke 12:2-3
[19] Philippians 3:4-6

he had known before Christ, all that he had lived before knowing Christ — as trash when compared to being new in Christ.[20]

Then God gave Paul two more gifts: some astonishing visions and a thorn in his flesh. [21] How many times have I heard preachers and people speculate what that 'thorn' was? Some of my favorites were epilepsy, an unsupportive wife he left at home, shameful memories, and simply: pains in his side.

Who cares? The 'thing' is not the point. Sorry.

If God wanted us to know, He would have told us. Let's focus on what God told us. Then let's ask, "What is this about?"

Does God's Word give us any insight? Yes. No matter how much of a "man of God" Paul was, he still had an issue to deal with, or maybe "it dealt with him." Paul said, "to keep me from becoming conceited."[22] Did the thorn keep Paul focused on God? Did he have to ask God to keep his thorn from taking over his life? I think so. God says gently to us all, "However spiritual you think you have become, I will leave a thorn in each of you."

He has placed a thorn in each of our sides. What has plagued us in the past, can and will plague us here and in the future all the way to that day when Christ fully redeems us in Heaven.

No matter how much we have grown, how much we have matured, something pricks us continually reminding us, "My thorn is still here. I must depend on God for everything today."

Dear friend, I know without asking. You have a thorn. So do I. We all do. And thank God for it. That thorn keeps me, keeps you humble before God. Some try to hide theirs by talking about how spiritual they are. They do so, knowing that at any time they could sin if they don't keep their eyes on Christ. When they don't, they sin. When I don't keep my eyes on Christ, I sin. Thankfully He is still there. He loves us, cares for us, and dusts us off to go

---

[20] Philippians 3:7-8
[21] 2 Corinthians 12:7
[22] 2 Corinthians 12:7

again, knowing that none of us will ever reach a place of *perfection*, sin free in this life.

Like Haggard's and my wrestling with the thorn, maybe you need to put down your precious image, and prized reputation and thank God for working in you, His child. Continually thank Him for daily shining His light, for letting the thorn work in us.

I laughed as an old evangelist friend told me of a friend whose reputation and image were being maligned. My friend told him, "That's what you get for having one!" Christian, it's all about Him, not you.

Again, looking through the lens of Paul's "outing" and thorn, what God did in Ted's life will prove to be beautiful if Ted is truly His child. Remember, we can't judge that Ted isn't His child.

This principle is good news to sinning friends — God had it in His plan.

It is all about God and the work He began in every believer's life.

Time comes to work in Ted's life, Paul's life, and in yours and mine,

Because He began and promised to finish His good work until we stand before Him.

Having watched preachers for years, and having studied God's Word, I believe that God only outs as publicly as He did Ted Haggard, Jim Baker, Jimmy Swaggart, Richard Roberts and other high-profile preachers when they deny their thorn. As they deny their painful, thorny reminders, they refuse to be humble before God. They then work to impress us that they're more spiritually perfect than they really are.

Life is all about God and the work He has begun in every believer's life. Never lose sight of this regardless of what life deals you. God doesn't love us because we are loveable, or have earned His love. He loves us because of Who He is.

It is time to frame the most important Bible verse for my thinking in this book. Here are two translations.

God's Word Says [23]	
[I am] confident of this, that He who began a good work in you will carry it on to completion until the day of Christ Jesus. (NIV)	There has never been the slightest doubt in my mind that the God who started this great work in you would keep at it and bring it to a flourishing finish on the very day Christ Jesus appears. (Message)

In a believer's life, God has told us, and this is worth putting it on your bathroom mirror so that you see it daily — He starts His work in us and will continue until the day Christ returns. God will complete you. God plans to finish the good work that He began in you when you first believed.

It's All about Him. (I.A.A.H.)

Well, Who Really Directs The Show?

Now, we say, "It is all about God."

We sing and we praise Him together, "It is all about God."

But we are ambivalent, even schizophrenic on this point. We think quietly, "it is all about us", as we have been taught and reinforced for years.

Christians are ambivalent. Again, Oswald Chambers is my most trusted devotional writer, but read this carefully: [24] "By Sanctification the Son of God is formed in me, *then I have to transform my natural life into a spiritual life.*"

See the inconsistency? It looks like my mentor is stuck in an inconsistency — God forms what He alone can form in me, *and then I have to transform* the rest? The only consistent way to say

---

[23] Philippians 1:6 (NIV) on the left, and the Message on the right.
[24] Ibid. March 18

it is: "God forms the new work in us and God continues to transform us."

Paul warned of this schizophrenic struggle this way. Read it in two translations.

God's Word Says [25]

Are you going to continue this craziness?	Are you so foolish?
For only crazy people would think they could complete by their own efforts what God began. If you weren't smart enough or strong enough to begin it, how do you suppose you could perfect it?	After beginning with the Spirit, are you now trying to attain your goal by human effort?

God and God alone finishes *our* amazing work. He begins it and just as He promises, He finishes it. Do you believe you can do anything, one small thing beyond what God is doing in you? No way.

But then Chambers says, *"I have to cleanse myself from all filthiness of the flesh and spirit until both are in accord with the nature of God."* [26] Again, see how Chambers places the Spirit's work on us?

We can't do more than God has worked "in" us. He is at work in us. (Have I said, "Just as He said?") If we could transform or grow ourselves, why would He need to pledge to work in us? Why would God need to assure us that He would continue His work until the end of our lives? Further, if we were perfect as religion pressures us to be, this work that God promises to *finish* wouldn't be needed. Finishing His work is His plan. Rest in it.

---

[25] Galatians 3:3-5 The Message is on the left, and the NIV is on the right.
[26] Ibid. March 18.

We must face the fact that we are no more of a match for the "tempter" than Ted Haggard was. Such a leader was no match, and if we think we are, we will always fall prey to Satan's snares. Paul put it this way, "By the grace given me I say to every one of you: 'Do not think of yourself more highly than you ought, but rather think of yourself with sober judgment, in accordance with the measure of faith God has given you.'"[27]

When we trust what God is doing in us and cling to Him to complete it, we can have the deep peace Scripture promises.[28] We do fine. But when we try to be gods, we fail. We have regrets. We want to go back in time and make it better.

We can't, but the world lies to us. It says we can fix anything. It coos that we can make up for past mistakes. Really, we can only see the past for what it was. Ask God's forgiveness for those we have failed or hurt, and remain humble in spirit before our loving Father.

A popular documentary has sucked in people who don't know God's Word. *The Secret*[29] purports a 'power in positive thinking'. Using this power we can be like gods. We can heal ourselves of cancer and prosper by just thinking we're wealthy. *The Secret* makes it all about us. It leads people in a direction diametrically opposed to God's Word. It plays to our lusts for riches and power rather than to desire God.

> **God told Jeremiah:** [1]
>
> Let not the wise man
> boast of his wisdom
> or the strong man
> boast of his strength
> or the rich woman
> boast of her riches,
> but let him who boasts —
> boast about this:
> that he understands
> and knows Me,
> that I am the Lord,
> Who exercises kindness,
> justice and
> righteousness on earth.

---

[27] Romans 12:3
[28] Romans 5:1 & 8:6
[29] Rhonda Byrne, (2004). *The Secret*. Prime Time Productions, Melbourne, Australia.

Moreover, *The Secret* has "Christian" devotees in the Faith Movement. With their eyes off God, they seek riches and fame. They teach a power in positive talking or speaking. They teach that we are like gods by what we 'speak out'.[30] According to some speakers, Creflo Dollar being one of the most vocal, we become wealthy by speaking it out; become healed by speaking to the illness; we can be and have anything just by our words. Forget, these people say, what is God's beautiful plan for our lives. Go after what the world craves.

A child of God will commit to God's wondrous plan for his or her life, whether it includes the riches of this world or whether it doesn't. Why? Because He is at work in us, precisely as He promised to bring about His plan.

Again, many of these teachings (you *can* have it all) take Christians in the opposite direction from where God leads us. Remember Jesus: "Seek first His kingdom and then He will add the other things."[31] We often want the world's stuff first. That makes it hard, but we will be able to seek first what God says as He builds His ability in us to follow Him first.

Think of it. Any teaching majoring on what we want rather than what God wants for us is like the 'New Age'.[32] It is sorcery, our wish to bend the world to our desires and positive thoughts, and it is inconsistent with God's teachings. It exists for the purpose of "getting, getting, and getting".

So we can't speak it and make it right. We can't go back and change the past, and if we can't go back, then what do we do? Jesus says, "You're asking the wrong question. You're looking for someone to blame. There is no such cause-effect here. Look

---

[30] Creflo Dollar is a well-known Word of Faith speaker. He teaches this in a documentary. www.creflodollarministries.org
[31] Matthew 6:33; Luke 12:31
[32] As reported in the *Secret* documentary.

instead for what God will do. Look for what God is doing, using all of our experiences, not wasting any of them."[33]

Look *forward*. First for the Jews and now for all Christians, God has always pushed us to look forward. Look downstream to His completing us! We let go of the past, and go forward in order to see "It's All About Him!"

What is the difference? Let me illustrate.

Learning to Dance!

Our daily walk with Christ is much like a dance. As you know, when a couple dances there can only be one leader. If both try to lead they create confusion and disharmony. If both try to lead, no one sees any 'dance'.

I saw this when my fiancé, Lanna, played a song for me, "Love Changes Everything." She wanted to play it for our first dance at the wedding reception.

I told her, "Get a choreographer for us. This can be a beautiful first dance."

A friend referred her to Jimmy, whose dark, short-cropped hair and build somehow made him even smoother. He was so poised. We told him we so wanted him to choreograph our "first dance" to that song — in ten days. He smiled and said, "No way. Not in ten days!"

I insisted we could. Our instructor insisted we could not.

I asked him to check his calendar. I was willing to pay him even if he said we could not do this. I asked him to see how many lessons he could work in over the next ten days.

He came back from his appointment book and said, "Look, I can give you ten hours, one session a day, but that will never be

---

[33] John 9:1-4

enough for you to accomplish, well, to accomplish what is not accomplishable."

I assured him that we could. If he did his amazing job, we would do ours and everything would turn out fine.

His response: "It's your money. If you want to waste it, let's get started."

He couldn't leave it there, "You know, couples come here and work for two to three months to prepare for such a dance —." He paused, "Even if you came twice a day —."

I looked at the "Always Dancing" sign and wondered. I saw we would dance on concrete here, and we would be dancing on concrete at the reception. He told us to wear shoes close to what we would be wearing, if not the same shoes. Shaking his head, he walked by some nondescript chairs over to the CD player and Jimmy listened to "Love Changes Everything." He walked through some steps, listened, walked through some more steps, listened and put his thoughts together about what would work well.

Now it was our turn.

That first night after a long day at work, still wearing what we wore to work, Lanna and I began to move on a thousand square feet and we watched ourselves in the mirrors.

Jimmy told us to keep our eyes on each other, and he would give us times to look out in the crowd. That was great, because we both loved looking at each other!

How did we progress?

We went backward first. We grew increasingly disappointed. Jimmy was frustrated at being right about the wrong thing — we wouldn't make it.

Days ticked by.

After two lessons, I told Lanna, "We have a problem, but it's one that we can solve. We have two options — you lead or I lead."

I told her, "You must follow me, or I can follow you — and you can choose. I'm okay either way."

It was a sticky moment. Her choice.

Lanna says she was thinking, "Wow." I am so in love with this guy. And by all indications, he is so in love with me. It was as though we were there to hold hands, put our arms around each other, and move about the room. It wasn't a chore."

She continues, "Gary was so sweet. He was such a gentleman — smooth, understanding, loving. Our lessons themselves were as memorable as the dance at the wedding reception. I felt so, so, special and loved. I was floating. And when he mentioned, 'One of us is going to lead.' *I didn't know I was not letting him lead!*"

Lanna says, "It was the prelude for the beautiful dance of our life."

She smiled and said, "You lead."

From that point, Lanna and I made incredible progress, largely because I started to lead, once she said for me to do so. She began to dance, attempting as she said, to let her partner lead.

I still had to stop dead still on the dance floor at times while Lanna danced on, me waiting until she came back! She failed in her first attempt to follow, but as I continued to stop unexpectedly for her to return, she led less and less, and finally, she was following and you could not see me leading. It was so subtle. As Lanna learned to give up control on the dance floor for this dance, we began to bond. We moved as one. It was beautiful, but I could only lead when she allowed me to do so.

After four lessons, I missed two nights. Lanna danced with Jimmy filling in for me, he told us that he had students that had taken lessons for over two months, and they would love to be where we were in one week.

Now we danced as one. When Lanna surrendered with each step, we grew together at so fast a pace that we amazed our instructor. How beautiful that evolving dance was to us! And you know what? I can't describe the bonding, the beauty that we enjoyed in that moment. That came to us as an unexpected serendipity. I cannot describe to you how beautiful she was dancing there.

Such serendipitous bonding with God surprises us. It continuously astounds us as we follow, as we obey a sovereign God on life's dance floor. All of heaven watches, and God, what does He say?

> He thought of everything,
> provided for everything we could possibly need,
> letting us in on the plans
> He took such delight in making.
> He set it all out before us in Christ,
> a long-range plan in which everything
> would be brought together and
> summed up in Him,
> everything in deepest heaven,
> everything on planet earth.
> It's in Christ that we find out
> who we are and what we are living for.
> Long before we first heard of Christ and
> got our hopes up, He had his eye on us,
> had designs on us for glorious living,
> part of the overall purpose He is working out
> in everything and everyone.
> It's in Christ that you,
> once you heard the truth and believed it,
> found yourselves home free—
> signed, sealed, and delivered by the Holy Spirit.
> [He] is God's signet
> the first installment on what's coming,
> a reminder that we'll get all God has planned for us,
> a praising and glorious life. [34]

When dancing with God becomes first in our lives, His Kingdom becomes more important than this world's stuff. Unlike

---

[34] Ephesians 1:8-17 (MSG)

what we see in *The Secret*, amazing Christians follow God so deftly that they look totally free.

The world sneers, and we are tempted to follow it, to seek what we want, to lead in our lives, to keep anyone from having control over us. The world can only study "up river" to explain who it says we were and therefore are. Using therapy and counseling, the world can only look back in time. The Bible teaches that we can go forward by learning new steps together with the Lord leading us into His future for us. And yes, like Lanna did in our first lessons, we will all keep on dancing to our own lead when God has stopped. He will patiently wait until we return to Him. But He is using even those silly, lonely steps by ourselves to grow us, to teach us, just as Lanna was learning on the dance floor.

As we focus on the beauty of what He is doing in us, we see more of His beauty in all things, in all that happens in our lives. He uses everything to grow us. We see Him lead. We see His beauty.

Think how often we rely on only one person to lead a dance for us. We don't want our surgical team to waste time while we lie on an operating table discussing "Who will lead in this surgery?" Let the lead surgeon lead! So for us, let the Great Physician lead.

Again, you don't want your cruise ship's crew arguing in a storm to see "Who can lead?" Let the captain lead in the storm. Let the Captain of our Fate lead.

Imagine the chaos with no generals, coaches, or lead engineers. We rely on leaders with wisdom, with experience, with the big picture to lead teams that obediently work as one under him or her.

With God and us, it comes down to His leading our dance. Just as Oswald Chambers writes,

"God took you up
into His purpose

by the Holy Ghost.

He is using you now
for His purposes
throughout the world
Just like He used His Son
for the purpose of our salvation.

"If you seek great things for yourself
"'God has called me for this and that'
you are putting a barrier
to God's use of you. *

"As long as you hold to your personal interest
Your self-developed character, or
Your set ambition,
You won't get identified with God's interest.

"You only arrive there by losing forever
any idea of your 'self' and
by letting God take you into His purpose for His world.
Even with that,
your paths are of the Lord,
so you may never understand your ways.
God is in control and He will lead us each step of the way."

> *We haven't the control to put up a roadblock or prevent God's design from coming to fruition.*
> Oswald Chambers

Think of it this way. Without this idea, we can't go forward in this book.

> It's not all about worship.
> It's not all about wisdom.
> It's not all about winning souls.
> — It's all about Him. There is no other dance.
> It's not about how many people you feed.
> It's not about how many gifts you gave to the needy.
> It's not about how many books you've written.
> It's not about how many staff members you have.
> It's not about how many attend the weekly services.
> — It's all about Him.
> *We have no other Dance Partner.*
> We've only one other option: our own filthy works.

4

IT'S ALL ABOUT HIM.
(I.A.A.H.)

An old joke may bring God's sovereignty as Creator and us as creatures into sharper focus.

Some scientists challenged God to a man-making contest. The scientists were so sure they could begin with raw materials and end up with a living person that they showed up on the chosen field at noon. Their labs were standing by. The field's green grass was cool in the autumn sun.

God showed up and was casual and friendly. The scientists showed profound pride in facing Him.

The scientists said, "Go" and both they and God scooped up dirt from the field.

At that point God smiled and pointed a finger at the scientists chuckling. He said, "No, no. Now you boys go get your own dirt. All this dirt is Mine. I made it."

God made it from nothing. "Spoke it," to be more exact, into existence.

The Bible's first verses[35] sing it out often: God said "it" — and "it" was. The "it" He spoke out was in turn seas, sky, stars, and mountains. You see it; He called it forth from nothing. And God made us.

God made us just as He wanted us to be.

God knew us before we were in our mothers' wombs.[36]

God made Adam and Eve just as He wanted them to be.

---

[35] Genesis 1:3, 6, 9, 11, 14, 20
[36] Psalm 139:13

No mistakes. None. Ponder this. We had absolutely nothing to do with how we were created, the womb we were put in, the family we had, our earliest surroundings or whether we were reared in church or not.

We are creatures, and infinitely above us and above our understanding, God remains the Creator.

So, if I am a creature, and God is Creator, how can I understand God's Sovereignty?

How can I understand God's Sovereignty?

More specifically, how can I understand it and not be afraid? I grow weary of preachers pushing me to believe God's sovereignty *based on fear*.

Do bad things happen? Yes. Have they happened to me? Yes. Do they happen to everyone? Yes.

Do I have any reason to walk through life timidly, afraid, or anxious? A thousand times "No!" Why not? I serve a Sovereign God and He has my life, all of it, in His hands. My life started that way and will always be in His hands. Either God is in control or we are. What we think about Who is in control doesn't change a thing.

Let's take some puzzles apart and look at them. These pieces show us God's sovereignty.

In the last two chapters we looked at two of them: time and justification. Both are God's playgrounds. He owns them both completely. We enjoy both, and command neither.

But look at God. God is Beautiful, and His beauty shows His sovereignty.

First, God is Beautiful.

I have stepped out of a car in Colorado, taken in the cold air and the blue green of evergreen-shrouded valleys crowned by white peaks and eye-aching blue above. For a minute the chill wind passed right through me. I felt small, blessed, alive, and fleetingly quick in passing before God's mountains, and I saw that God's creation is beautiful. But there is more to it than that.

He is beautiful.

God is beautiful. Few people have glimpsed God, but all said He was majestically beautiful: Moses[37] saw the tail of God's presence and it burned a radiance on his face that people could not bear to see for a month! Isaiah[38] was struck by his own filth on seeing God. Peter[39], John[40], and Paul[41] were all changed enough by seeing God that they lived for Him and willingly died for Him.

Moses was stunned by God's love and spent most of the time that God passed by with his face planted on rock. Watching God overwhelmed him. Isaiah could not take in God's grandeur without sensing his own filth in comparison to God's beauty! Peter never escaped God's haunting, soul-penetrating voice! John gave up trying to describe God's glory when he realized all the books in the world could not come close.[42] And Paul. Paul tried all of his life to describe the glory — the beauty he had witnessed.

Get this. The beauty of the red-orbed sun setting on a beach is nothing compared to the One Who spoke into existence both that sun and the rolling waves crashing on that sandy beach.

We love these beauties:

Wheat fields as far as you can see —

Woods so thick you can only see up tree canyons to catch patches of cloud and blue —

A volcano's exploding red cauldron against a backdrop of wavering stars —

And none of these compare to God's beauty Who made all of the beauty that you love.

---

[37] Exodus 34:5ff.
[38] Isaiah 6:1ff
[39] 2 Peter 1:18ff
[40] Revelation 1:1 ff, 4:1ff
[41] 2 Corinthians 12:2ff
[42] John 21:25

Should I fear such stunning beauty? Shouldn't I trust God Who authors such beauty? Hollywood gets us to trust and identify with beautiful actors in movies, whose real lives are violent wrecks — but God has an unblemished beauty, a beauty we can trust.

But the mountains' beauty holds an unyielding, granite coldness. Wander in them without adequate protection, food, water, and maps, and inevitably terrible things happen. Mountains' beauty is stark. So also the beauty of beaches, forests, and volcanoes — all have dangers.

So God must not just be beautiful. He must also be gracious. He is. He showed us by sending His Son. We promptly crucified Him according to God's plan and purpose, and God resurrected Jesus back — not to Heaven *but to us* — to conquer death for us! "Grace" is a theological category beyond any law, beyond justice, and far beyond mere mercy: God did the unexplainable. We call God's action grace.

So God's beauty is clothed in gracious kindness to us, in His undeserved care for us.

Why we trust Him

As we see God's beauty and grace — we can trust Him. But preachers paint a God whose sovereignty is controlling, fearful, demanding, and changing His mind; which pushes us to a huge, yawning chasm! On one side preachers paint God's severe sovereignty, and on the chasm's other side they show our loving Father. It's as if the severe God of the Old Testament grew up between the Old and New Testament and had a Son and become the God we trust!

I was fortunate to come to God's *rule* first through seeing His kindness, His undying devotion to me. Coming to God's *dominion* through His eternal security for me as a believer gave me a wonder-filled vantage point to see God. I was fortunate to trust God's *sovereign rule* as loving and gracious in 1969. I first came to God's dominion as unshakably invested in my completion — [43] "that the God who started this great work in me would keep at it and bring it to a flourishing finish on the very day Christ Jesus appears!"

How do you see God's sovereignty?

Try a little test. Consider that we are at your favorite coffee shop and talking. You feel safe, so I ask you, "What is your first reaction to God's sovereignty?" I then say, "and may I ask you what is your second, your third, and your fourth response to God's sovereignty?"

So, whichever is your first reaction, then number it "1" and whichever might be second: "2". If none of these are your first reaction, then write in yours and put it as "1" in the list! But put down your four strongest reactions. Rank them 1-4.

____ Worship. I fall down recognizing His kingship, His "right to everything" and His Lordship.

____ Fear. It just shoots through me how awesome, fearful, immense and powerful He is.

____ Submission. I acquiesce to His will for my life, for the world.

____ Trust. I know He's good. He's great, *and* He's good.

____ Risk. God often does not reveal His providence before I must act. So, I must risk.[44]

____ Completion. I trust He is going to finish His work in me.

____ Saved. His will is to redeem me.

____ Loved. So great a God has proven His love to me.

____ I feel _____

How did you arrange your responses? Did you rank fear(s) or the love and grace responses higher?

Look at how God is committed to us as believers. What can separate us from a mighty God's love?

- ♥ **No One** shall separate us.[45] If you could "remove" yourself from God's protection, then that would put you in control of

---

[43] Philippians 1:6 (MSG)
[44] Risk would otherwise be terribly frightening.
[45] Romans 8:35

your corner of the universe, not God. I believed that for so long. How miserable I was before I came to trust God's control of everything. Now I know.

No 'one' can drive a wedge between you and Christ's love for you including you! There is no way!

♥ **No Thing** shall separate us.[46]
neither death nor life,
neither angels nor demons,
neither the present nor the future,
nor any powers,
neither height nor depth,
nor anything else in all creation,
will be able to separate us from the love of God that is in Christ Jesus our Lord.

So how did I come to trust God's inalterable Hand in our world, in my life?

Pure Form of Election

Years ago I saw an ad in the *Tulsa World* for an all day Saturday seminar taught by a man named Bob Enyart. His subject intrigued me: God's Sovereignty. I was drawn to it. I decided to attend. I talked my son into going with me and laughed as we entered the doors to find we weren't meeting in the sanctuary but in the basement. As Enyart spoke, I sensed why we were sequestered in the basement!

My attending was no accident. God was leading my life. I was ready to hear this teaching, or I

> For those God foreknew He also predestined to be conformed to the likeness of his Son, that [Jesus] might be the firstborn among many brothers. And those He predestined, He also called; those He called, He also justified; those He justified, He also glorified. What, then, shall we say in response to this? If God is for us, who can be against us?

---

[46] Romans 8:38-39

wouldn't have felt drawn to attend. Looking back, it was a turning point in my life.

Sitting in the basement and learning how God elects Christians to salvation, along with God's sovereignty — was the craziest stuff I had ever heard. We finished at four in the afternoon, and I wondered why I had spent the entire day.

The next week, I was sharing the day and my reaction with an evangelist friend when he surprised me. He didn't think the teaching was crazy, and he didn't take my bait to laugh with me. His reaction surprised me. I was shocked. He fully believed it! I told him that I had never heard him preach anything close to this and he replied: "Gary, I go into churches for three-night revivals. There is no way I could preach this in that setting. It would be like force-feeding steak to babies."

Now I was stunned. One teacher was a fluke. But a teacher and now a trusted friend forced me to turn and study this issue. It completely went against what I thought of God. Let that soak in. Election, the fact that God chose those to be saved, flew in the face of the way I defined God, but I had to believe it after several months of studying His Word. I came to see that election was woven throughout The Bible.

What I mean by the pure form of election is simply that God chose those that will be saved.

Not only does God *know* as most believe, He's also actually *chosen them* as many do not believe. See the beauty: whether one believes this or not doesn't change your eternal accommodations if he or she is a child of God. It only helps them see God's plan in their lives.

I haven't talked to anyone who truly came to this without personally studying God's Word on the issue. It is too foreign to what we think we know of God or His love.

Something amazing happened as I read God's Word, focusing on His electing us. I can't explain this and doubt anyone else can. I don't even understand it nor do I have a driving need to make anyone else see it — you see, I still see God as love even when I see that He created those that won't be chosen. Why? I don't know. I don't need to understand. I only know that His Word says, "He already knew His people and had already appointed them to have the same form as the image of His Son."[47]

This truth points me to scriptures telling us that His ways are not our ways, our wisdom is foolishness to Him, and His wisdom is foolishness to our natural thinking. He is God and I trust Him, even in this. I trust my understanding to Him when and wherever He chooses — if ever.

Those who can't quite go this far stop at believing that God only *knows* who the ones that will be saved are. I won't attempt an extensive scripture presentation of why I came to believe this, but let me say that I read it, prayed about it, meditated on it, and came to accept it. Also, as I said, God has a plan for all His children: a specific plan. So, with that as a starting place, I saw that the Bible taught this. God full well knew who would accept Him. As I have said, He chose them.

Here is part of the Bible's trail for this truth.

The Death Of Jesus —

In Jerusalem "there gathered together against Your holy servant Jesus, Herod and Pilate, the Gentiles and the Jews, to do whatever Your hand and Your purpose predestined to occur." [48]

Our Salvation

> "Those [God] foreknew, God also predestined to become conformed to the image of His Son, that Jesus might be the first-born among many brethren; and whom God predestined."[49]
>
> "God predestined us to adoption as sons and daughters through Jesus Christ to Himself, according to the kind intention of His will."[50]

---

[47] Romans 8:29 God's Word Translation.
[48] Acts 4:27-8
[49] Romans 8:29-30
[50] Ephesians 1:5

Knowing Anything About God

"We speak God's wisdom in a mystery, the hidden wisdom, which God predestined before the ages to our glory."

Our Assurance of Salvation in Christ Jesus.

"We have obtained an inheritance, having been predestined according to His purpose Who works all things after the counsel of His will."[51]

The Scriptures also clearly tell me that we can only come to Christ when He draws us. "No one can come to Me [Jesus] unless the Father who sent Me draws him." [52] Now no one in my understanding, could ever resist His drawing: no one. I simply can't imagine anyone who has been embraced by God's astounding love refusing Him! So Jesus said we never come to Him on our own — God draws us.

If a revelation doesn't move you to Him, it's not enough. It might be part of His drawing, but His drawing is always successful even when we are in disobedience.

Now I fully recognize that:
1) It feels harsh to think that I didn't have something to do with my coming to Christ.
2) Unlearning as Chambers called it is a hard start to learning.
3) None of us know all there is to know or have God's pure truth.
4) This opposes all I was taught as a child and in college. It opposes what my father taught, and what many in my denomination believe.

My question is simply, "Have you studied God's Word on this with an open heart and spirit? Have you prayed for God to reveal His truth to you?"

Again, God elected me. He began His work in me long before I was aware of Him. I now see many ways He was drawing

---
[51] Ephesians 1:11
[52] John 6:44

me to Himself before I gave my life to Him in February of 1966. Okay, that was my story, but what of others' stories?

How is it that one person comes to Christ and another doesn't? Again, we return to the issue: "Is it about us, or Him?" I ask again, "Could anyone intentionally resist Christ and all that He has to offer?"

When wrestling with this, I pointed to conditions in people's lives: apathy, bitterness, alcoholism, and abuse for starters. But then I saw that other men and women suffering in those same conditions heard the Truth and professed Christ as Lord. Why is it that the ones who respond to God, reacted differently than the ones sitting next to them hearing the same message? Again, is that about *them* rather than God? This issue goes back to Adam and Eve's situation. Adam and Eve did nothing more than be used by God to bring about His beautiful plan.

Start in the Garden

How ridiculous we've been to blame Adam and Eve. How many preachers have you heard teach that Adam and Eve were at fault for sin being in the world?

Examine the biblical record: "Sin entered the world through one man, and death through sin, and in this way death came to all men, *because all sinned*."[53] The Bible does not make Adam the "fall guy." It simply records the facts. On the face of it, there was no "fall" so there wasn't a "fall guy."

Sin entered at this point. What point? The point where God had created Satan, put Adam and Eve in the Garden, and moved off stage for the serpent to tempt them.

God alone created them. He alone put them where He wanted them. He put in them the desires, needs, and drives that He purposed — they chose none of those. Then God Himself put an

---

[53] Romans 5:12

'off limits' tree *in the middle* of their world,[54] knowing everything from the beginning. God designed and knew their thought processes. He designed and knew Satan who would tempt them. And God knew the outcome, even that of Jesus coming to die.[55]

With all of this in mind, my question to you is: "Were Adam and Eve rebellious? Were they sinning? Or did God have a plan — beautiful for their lives and all our lives?" God tells us, "As the heavens are higher than the earth, so are My ways higher than your ways and My thoughts than your thoughts."[56]

God watched the forbidden fruit being eaten. That didn't surprise Him, did it? No —

- Did God put the wrong people in the garden?
- Had God picked stronger people, would they not have rebelled?
- Had Adam and Eve had any teaching about what sin was? Or what sin would really cost?
- As God draws people to Himself, whether in churches or bars, they are all equal, except — He elected some of them.

Look further at Adam and Eve. When they were still in the Garden with God, He covered them supernaturally, though they were not physically covered. Their nakedness was natural, lovely. When they chose the apple, sinned and discovered that they were not covered — they knew something entirely new to them — fear. How strange it must have felt for the first time! How awful its shame must have burned them!

Had their former trust in God fled? Did their sin bring fear unnecessarily? As they grew aware that they were physically uncovered, God had a plan of love and mercy, *covering them*

---

[54] Genesis 2:9
[55] Rev. 13:8 "All whose names have not been written in the book of life belonging to the Lamb that was slain from the creation of the world."
[56] Isaiah 55:9

physically by using animal skins.[57] They had already sewn laughable coverings from fig leaves,[58] but God served them. He replaced their laughable attempts at camouflage clothing out of His Great Love!

God even created in them what caused them to react as they did after eating the apple. How else would they have had any such reaction in them? Yet throughout history we have been taught that Adam and Eve were responsible for sin coming into existence. How ridiculous. That would make them creators. Do you believe they decided how creation would be? Worse, did they in their own power cause all that God had planned to be changed?

No matter what Adam and Eve did, God covered them: physically and supernaturally. God covered them. In His Garden, but out of His presence, they were already covered by the next part of God's beautiful plan. God provided access to Himself outside the Garden.[59]

So why did they fear? Why did they hide? He provided for and took care of their choices because He had a plan. No direction, no outcome was based on them being in control of what they did. It was all part of God's plan.

> "It is said that in some countries trees will grow, but will bear no fruit because there is no winter there." John Bunyan (1628-1688)

I know that some Scriptures fly in the face of election, and I can't answer them all. I only know that I didn't come to a conviction about election until I studied it, disagreed with it, fought it, and searched the Bible again while asking God to show me truth. Then I came to this rock. I won't judge those that do not agree. I will conclude that on this issue I do not agree with them, or they with me, knowing that this is no requirement, according to God's Word, to

---

[57] Genesis 3:21
[58] Genesis 3:7
[59] Genesis 4:4ff

make it into Heaven. That is Christ, faith in Christ alone, praise God.

I could spend much more space on this subject as both sides have filled thousands of books debating it. I can only witness to the fantastic change it has made in my life. I have only one concern. How shall we then live? What difference does it make in us, and how we live when we "get" God's sovereignty?

Transformers: All to Beauty!

When we trust God's plan for us, when we trust His ability to prosecute His plan for us, then *all* of our experiences have a new beauty. Why? Because *we know* God is using all our experiences to make us more like Him.

What makes His plan beautiful to me? No wasted time. No wasted experiences. I grew up loving the old Gospel song "Wasted Years" until I came to see there aren't any!

We can look back on all our experiences and look forward to all of them and *know* that He was, that He is, and that He will be in control. God's love for us is in back of His plan. His love for us is its foundation.

"Every move I make, every breath I take" is secure when God is sovereign.

You can now know you are going through what you are supposed to go through. Ask yourself, "How could I ever live being 'anxious for nothing'[60] if I didn't believe this?"

When you grasp this, you see Christ through new eyes. Remember, Christ sought no attention for Himself; it was all about the Father! Jesus did not seek to share God's glory; Jesus left God's glory with God.[61] When God *desired to honor* Jesus, He did so gloriously.[62]

---

[60] Philippians 4:6-7
[61] Philippians 2:6-7
[62] Matthew 3:17 & 17:15

What's more, even the sins in our lives are tools to be used of God. Again, coming to see this as God's truth allows you to live a life where you aren't "anxious" when you fail, when you sin. Sin is part of what happens in life as God grows you.

Consider this. If I fall to a sin: sloth, lust, anger, pride, envy, gluttony, and greed— Okay, *when* I fall to a deadly sin the game is not over. No! See this. Each of those sins teaches an opposing virtue. God uses sin to show me *where I am* — in an ugly, deathly place. God also uses sin to show me *where I'm not*! Look at how the opposing virtues build God's character in us!

Where I am	Where I'm not but want to be!
Sloth	**Diligence:** I do what is important, what is good, what succeeds.
Lust	**Love:** I seek to build up God's high value in a person.
Anger	**Patience:** My faith in God's timely providence is unshakable.
Pride	**Humility:** I breathe in, I depend on God's grace.
Envy	**Contentment:** I trust God's provision to me is in His plan.
Gluttony	**Wisdom:** I seek always to accomplish God's highest good.
Greed	**Generosity:** I sacrifice my wants to give to God's work.

Do you see? In believers, even sin is part of God's sovereign, beautiful plan to complete us. Sin always points to its opposing virtue!

Christians Who Teach Fear

Most preachers and Christians live a response and teach a response I can only characterize as "consistently inconsistent".

Preachers preach God's sovereignty, but throw in fear, thus becoming inconsistent. God is gracious, loving and sovereign — no inconsistency. Why do preachers wedge a fear motivator into their message of God's sovereignty?

At least those who follow the teachings of Arminius[63] are consistent. Their doctrine holds fear, because salvation depends on their responses, on their efforts, on their goodness.

Fear creeps in to taint, even dominate our Christian gospel. Both those who stress man's freedom and those who sound God's sovereignty show strong fear strands. Calvinists, who teach a believer's eternal security based on God's strong sovereignty, should proclaim His beauty and grace more loudly!

Calvinists shout God's saving power and His grace covering all their sins, but once that is established, they then slip to teach fear almost as much as Arminian teachers.

Instead of fear and warnings, the Gospel, the Good news of Jesus comes with clear — what?

Not Warnings, but —

Look at someone I respect: [64] "a warning which needs to be reiterated is that the cares of this world, the deceitfulness of riches, and the lust of other things entering in, *will choke all* that God puts in."

I agree with my friend. But look at how he puts it. Why do writers slip a fear emphasis into God's Word? Take this. For example, "warning". Why warn so often? Warning is negative and has at its base: fear. God simply *informs* us how He works in us. Look at where the NIV says *warn* and look at the real words the Bible uses.

---

[63] Jacobus Arminius (1560-1609), a Dutch pastor and theologian, reacted to the predestination of the Reformers, saying that God's grace was more important than His Predestining believers, and leaving the responsibility for persevering with a saint, who could lapse in his faith.

[64] Oswald Chambers

The NIV uses the word "Warn"	Original Word(s) [65]
Jesus WARNED: Be careful, watch for [66]	TAKE HEED: *behold, attend to.*
[Jesus] remember that I WARNED you. [67]	TOLD: *speak, say.*
[Pentecost]: [Peter] WARNED them. [68]	TESTIFIED: *charge*
I never stopped WARNING each of you. [69]	WARN: *caution, reprove gently.*
... But WARN him as a brother. [70]	ADMONISH: *to put in my mind.*
I WARN you ... those who live like this will not inherit God's kingdom. [71]	TELL: *predict, tell beforehand*
WARN a divisive person, and WARN him a second time. After that — [72]	WARN: *caution, reprove*
I WARN all who hear these words. [73]	TESTIFY: *bear witness.*

Do you see how we take words that at face value tell, show, point out and corroborate but we then translate them to be fear-tinged like *warn*? Now we know we are surrounded by challenges, dangers, and sin.

We're never free from sin's recurring tides in us. Okay, but isn't life in Christ supposed to be exciting? Aren't we supposed to enjoy life in Christ? Even with trials, shouldn't it excite us? I am committed to your opening up to what I am sharing here so God

---

[65] The **Original** words are Greek words and their translations in Lexicons and how they were translated in the King James Version when literate people used more words.
[66] Mark 8:15
[67] John 16:4
[68] Acts 2:40
[69] Acts 20:31; 1 Corinthians 4:14; 1 Thessalonians 5:14
[70] 2 Thessalonians. 3:15
[71] Galatians 5:21
[72] Titus 3:10
[73] Rev. 22:18

can bring you to a place where you will enjoy this beautiful, this exciting walk with Him.

We know that money or lack of money; of friends or lack of friends; or difficult circumstances are parts of God's plan. God tells us all of these things happen. But lay off the fear. All these things happen in every life but they do not condemn us to live through them fearfully.

You wonder, "Would that be wonderful?" I can tell you it is and you can experience it as you unlearn the fear driven things you were taught.

And as you grasp God's sovereignty, fear and anxiety are banished.

Think of Parts of Your Life that God's Sovereignty Changes

Question: How can we ever have a peace that things, as tough as they are, are going exactly as God planned for them to happen — if He doesn't have the power and the plan?

How can we not be concerned or anxious over our circumstances, unless God knows them better than we do, and in our subconscious we trust Him and His plan?

Many trusted preachers and teachers are ambivalent, even schizoid toward God's sovereignty. They say, "God saves eternally. God is

> When Jeremiah and Isaiah wrote these "testimonies", God had promised both of them that their city would be burned to the ground, the leadership deported, and the dead would fill canyons — life would come "undone" in every way. And the horrors had begun. Now hear what God had them say to us.
>
> Jeremiah: *"I know the thoughts and plans that I have for you,"* says the Lord, *"thoughts and plans for welfare and peace and not for evil, to give you hope in your final outcome."*[1]
>
> Isaiah: *"Behold, all you who attempt to kindle your own fires [and work out your own plans of salvation], who surround and gird yourselves with momentary sparks, darts, and firebrands that you set aflame! —Walk by the light of your self-made fire and of the sparks that you have kindled for yourself, if you will)!*[1]

sovereign. God elects surely." But they warn us in fear-laced messages and place the onus on us.

Trust this, believer.
- ➢ Where you are can change any day,
- ➢ But you are exactly where God intended you to be,
- ➢ Today and tomorrow, God will use
- ➢ *Wherever you are* to continue His beautiful work in you.

We reject so much out of fear, but here is bedrock: all that happens in a Christian's life, everything is part of His plan to grow us.

So what are you praying, trusting, and doing where you are?

We have only begun to grasp the magnitude of His love.

Do you tell God what you will accept in your current situation?

Or have you begun trusting Him for what He has planned for you here?

Are you growing to agree with Him, and fully accept all that is happening as coming from His love for you? I wrestled with God's love over my fear(s) in my book, *Fear is Never Your Friend*. What a joy it is to come to His love!

Sovereignty is *so* practical.

5

LIMITS ON GOD?
YOU'RE KIDDING ME!

Ministers that I trust and others talk about how we limit God in our lives.

Question: How do Christians think they could ever limit God from doing *anything* He intends? After all, we are His bond slaves. He bought and paid for us. If we can limit God, doesn't that put us in control? How could we ever become what He desires for us if we could limit Him?

If we can limit God, then His plan going forward hinges on us. That brings profound pressure. Guilt and condemnation would sneak up and overwhelm us! We would continually be fearful as we asked ourselves, "Have I prayed enough?" "Okay, did I pray *believing*? Do I even know the right Scriptures?" Have I given enough? Served enough? Witnessed enough? Visited enough sick people or prisoners? No! I haven't!"

Of course, I have never done enough! I don't move God with my tears, fears, or score cards. I only *move* Him with my complete trust — trust in His plan, which unfolds in His sovereignty and Glory! And my ability to trust Him comes out of growth that he brought about in me.

I may motivate myself by fear and anxiety, but not as God desires and with no fruit or lasting joy. How often do we move ourselves in fear?

How often do we put ourselves in positions where everything depends on us? We then worry if we have achieved *enough*.

Were we responsible *enough*, accountable *enough*, good or smart *enough*? In this place we alternate between anxiety and fear of failure or we take *pride* in accomplishments! If we are stuck in *enoughs* it's still *all about us*. We *even tout our successes* so as to feel like we accomplish *something for God.* How quickly "It's about us", replaces "It's all about Him." When we rely on ourselves, we try to limit God.

I no longer believe we can limit God. Only God can choose to limit Himself, and even then, He is in control. Otherwise, we have more power over what goes on in our lives than He does. Many Christians believe we have such a power. I no longer do.

Along the same line of "it all depends on me," preachers hold out this promise: "The most important thing to you is that you should be so identified with the Lord that there is nothing of the old life left." Really? Where does the Bible say we will be perfect here on earth? Some of the old life, old nature, or sin will always be left in us. Sin will always be left in us and that is where God constantly works in us to conform us to His Son's image!

> We cannot discover our failure to keep God's law except by trying our very hardest (and then failing). Unless we really try, what ever we say there will always be at the back of our minds the idea that try if we harder next time we shall succeed in being completely good.
>
> Thus, in one sense, the road back to God is a road of moral effort, of trying harder and harder. But in another sense it is not trying that is ever going to bring us home. All this trying leads up to the vital point at which you turn to God and say, "You must do this. I can't."
>
> C. S. Lewis -from *Mere Christianity*

How often have I prayed, wept, and begged for all my "nature to" or desire to sin to be gone? No one experiences it *all gone*. Perfection lies only on death's other side when we are united with Jesus. I now trust that part of His gorgeous plan.

Since Adam and Eve, God has used our "nature to" sin in us to further His beautiful creation in us. Can you imagine life with no sin? Without sin that shows us that we need a Savior, helps us see where we are, and where we aren't? Sin drives us to Him continually. Sin constantly reminds us — we need God as our Savior, Redeemer. So, Thank God they ate the apple! [74]

I see another place where we make it all about us.

Christians fall into thinking, "We're saved by our *faith*." Really? God's work on the Cross saves us, not our faith. How could we possibly have faith until Christ comes into us?[75] What does the Bible say? "It is by grace you have been saved, through faith, *and this not from yourselves*, it is God's gift, not by works, so that no one can boast." [76]

Our imperfect faith is marred and twisted at best. God's grace must even cover our faith, so it reads "by grace through faith."

God saves us. He accomplishes it in Christ's cross. God manifests His grace to us in the faith He gives. Part of God's drawing us to Himself is manifested in the faith He gives us. His stunning plan to complete us is manifested in the faith God gives us.

The Beauty of One Yielded Life

I attended the funeral of a 22-year-old woman who lived a beautiful life — but not a life anyone would choose.

Her life touched so many that hundreds packed the large church and its balcony. The sun streaming through stained glass caught tears rolling down men's faces. I heard no coughing or shuffling. Many wore black for respect, while others wore colors as a joyous testimony. The funeral moved me, yet all of this was for someone who had not spoken a word since the age of two.

---

[74] Lewis, C. S. (2005). September 23rd "Leaving It to God" in *A Year With C.S. Lewis, Daily readings from His Classic Works*. Zondervan.
[75] Ephesians 2:8-9 Message
[76] Ephesians 2:8-9 (NIV)

The pastor began to speak, husky voiced. He was commanding and vibrant. His poignant sadness made the minutes powerful, meaningful, and persuasive. He began to speak of the 22-year-old woman and about her choices that she made. I wanted to yell out at that point.

I looked around. Something caught in my throat. My heart rate ramped up. I looked around again. Everyone else was still staring ahead at the pastor. I wanted to whisper to those around me, but dared not.

I wanted to stand and raise my objection, which I have done countless times in courtrooms that were far more intimidating. I did not.

That did it. I knew I had to write this chapter. I had to say it. Say it in writing. Say it unashamedly. Say it with total conviction. This young lady never chose to live her life like this — no one would! Who would choose such a life?

She made no choice, nor was she offered one to live her life as she had to live it. She had no voice in the matter, literally. She had no free will. If she had possessed any free choice it was abolished.

I won't criticize or judge the pastor. He did an outstanding job — saying what pastors have said through the ages. He repeated what's been said in thousands of churches for centuries. He preached as he was taught. He comforted with what his seminary gave him to give us in the pews. He was taught like the rest of us. How can we fault him? Again, it's time to unlearn.

It is time to know the Truth.

That is what this book is about. The Truth that boldly points out that it *is truly all about God. It is not about us.*

God is not here for us. We are here for Him.

God is no Heavenly Slot Machine.

God in His goodness and beauty, created her for His purpose, just as He has created all of us. Not for our purposes, but for His. She did not choose her purpose, would not have chosen it.

You did not choose yours, although you might have been tempted to choose parts of your life over the plight of millions of others' wretched lives.

For all of them and all of us, God bought us with a price, His death on a cross. He chose His believers. He elected us and He draws us to Himself in hearing His Word through ministers and His children in order to send us into His world to preach the gospel. That is all part of Plan A.

As we respond, and we will if we are His chosen, we become both children and bond slaves. Not Him for us, but us for Him.

Come to Him. Whether you believe it's your choice or His sovereignty, when chosen by God a transformation begins. We become His slaves. His Word so clearly tells us that! Bought and paid for with a terrible price —the stripes on His back and His death on a cross.

And, thankfully in His resurrection as His child and slave, God tells us that He orders our steps. Period.

Once we come to Him, scripture puts no condition on His ordering the steps of the righteous. No condition is based on our efforts (Are you *unlearning*?). Nowhere in God's Word does it say God orders the steps of those who cooperate with Him, or *let Him* lead them.

We are His to do with us as He pleases not as we please. Again, theologians try to put conditions on God, saying that *we* must cooperate, or *we* let Him do anything in us. Not so. God's Word does not say such.

> **How to walk with a Sovereign God?**
>
> In his heart a man plans his course, but the Lord determines his steps.
> Proverbs 16:9
>
> Devise your strategy, but it will be thwarted; propose your plan, but it will not stand, for God is with us.
> Isaiah 8:10
>
> "I know My plans for you," declares the Lord, "plans to prosper you and not to harm you, plans to give you hope and a future."
> Jeremiah 29:11

In the same way that our righteousness is not based on our works, or goodness, our righteousness *is* based on one thing, and one thing alone: Him and what He did for us at the cross.

Why is this so difficult to see and believe? We can't turn loose of feeling that we're in control. (Can you unlearn yet, so you can learn?)

Just as God created this 22-year-old for a purpose. She didn't choose her life as an invalid, unable to walk, talk, sing, play and move about. God did.

At the age of 2, a disease struck the child. She lived the balance of her life with no ability to do the things we enjoy. She was bed-ridden, communicating only with her eyes and limited body motions.

Was her life a blessing to all who came in contact with her? She never told a joke, nor dressed to impress anyone, or hugged them —and still, what a blessing.

Who did this? God did.

Why? He did it because of His love.

Can we understand that? No. Let that sink in. No. It's a mystery.

We can only know what He says in His Word, that He is love; always has been. Always will be to those who are part of His elect, His precious chosen one, and are presently or one day will be His bond slave.

Who directs your steps? Who ordered hers? The answer is simple. If you are His bond slave, bought and paid for with death on a cruel cross, then God directs your steps.

God always directs the steps of the righteous regardless of what we do. Why? Because our being righteous was what Jesus made us on the cross not something we purchase moment by moment! She could purchase no good works as we think of them.

A chill wind blew at her gravesite. I was surprised by as large a crowd as I have ever seen at a graveside. And she never went out, socialized, bowled, danced at a prom, led a cheer, or attended a Bible study. She communicated with no one outside those close to her who could read her body language.

God again used the pastor to move me at her graveside as he preached God's love: how He loved this woman. How He loved her more than any of us could ever love or understand.

And, yes, this was the life God chose for her, not one she chose for herself.

Will we ever understand? In her short life, did anyone understand how a loving God let this happen? I doubt it, but ask Him to enlarge your heart, and change your perspective. I know this. We'll never explain how a loving God accomplished *such beauty in her*. How did He use her to imprint such grace on so many standing in that day's chill wind? What a statement of God's mystery! Jesus told us to seize hold of God's purpose for today, rather than use theology to try and understand it![77]

We can understand as much as we see God for Who He is and see us for who we are: bond slaves for His purpose(s).

As I turned to walk from the gravesite through the crinkly white grass, the wind blew another man's words to me, "Nobody has touched so many lives."

Thank You, Jesus, for her life. Thank you, for her beauty and her grace in You. Thank You, Jesus, for providing a loving home to care for Your gift to so many, a family making so many sacrifices, a family showing so much love and patience that it would take another book to begin describing their love. And yet, even their love for her couldn't begin to register on a scale of Christ's Love for us!

I know as a parent, you would never choose to have a child live as this woman did, but what a blessing she was to her parents. I can tell you that they have missed her terribly. They grieved her passing from them. She was God's blessing. I know because that young lady's mother is my wife's sister.

---

[77] John 9:1-3

And I know countless parents of special children, and they see God's hand in their children's lives as this couple did.

I Respond: Beyond Circumstances

From Genesis to the end in Revelation, woven throughout scripture is God's great plan, His love for His children. Scholars have translated God's attributes to implement His plan. He is omniscient, omnipresent, and omnipotent (all-powerful and unstoppable). He is Supreme. The Bible says He knew us and set us aside before the earth's foundations.

Scripture commands us to be content in all our circumstances, which spiritually resides next door to *be anxious for nothing.*[78]

> For [God] chose us in Him before the creation of the world to be holy and blameless in His sight.
> Ephesians 1:4 (NIV)

Hear Paul: "I have learned to be content whatever the circumstances. I know what it is to be in need, and I know what it is to have plenty. I have learned the secret of being content in any and every situation, whether well fed or hungry, whether living in plenty or in want."[79] What do we get when we learn to rest in God no matter the circumstances? The next verse tells us: "I can do everything *through Him* who gives me strength."[80]

Christ of God is our Plan. Jesus is Our Key. The Son of Man is God's Provision. Christ at the right hand of God works on our behalf at this very moment. Our High Priest is working, building, moving, erecting, tearing down, creating, and changing everything in our lives — all for His great plan to be accomplished in our life. IAAH. (It *is* All About Him.)

---

[78] Philippians 4:6-7
[79] Philip. 4:11-12
[80] Philippians 4:13 (NIV)

God says, "I know what I'm doing. I have it all planned out—plans to take care of you, not abandon you, plans to give you the future you hope for."[81] As Jeremiah wrote God's beautiful promise, he was stuck in a frightening place. A siege drove people mad with hunger. Outside Jerusalem's protective walls, an army waited to kill any survivors. Disease ran rampant because they could not carry out their dead or wastes, and God promised Jeremiah: "I have you where you are. I am taking you where I desire, and it will be what you had hoped for."

Let me step aside and draw a distinction, please. What you hope for is reality, not circumstances. Let me explain. The car you drive is a circumstance. Your reality is to go where God directs and serve Him, to be blessed as He blesses. Any of a thousand cars will let you do that, so they are all circumstances to reality — *go as God directs*. Circumstances like fashions, stock markets and cars change continually. Reality only grows.

We live — really live — when we finally live "in" It's All About Him.

I Respond. I Give God 'Both Parts' of Me

Consider a simple, practical result of It's All About Him.

We divide our lives into two parts: a good part and a bad part. Our good part belongs to God. He uses and increases it. We ask Him to bless the good things in it. We ask Him to use us as we do good things in the good part. We then have a bad part. And we ask Him to forgive things in the bad part, and we then want to forget them. If God can forget them, then we want to as well, and move on. We forget them, moving out of their bondage as we forgive ourselves as God forgave us. But God knew and purposed both parts — good and bad — to instruct us in His beautiful plan.

---

[81] Jeremiah 29:11 (MSG)

Like the 22-year-old woman, you never chose this. Couldn't God have made you perfect when you came to Him? He is both our Creator and the Author of our re-creation. Are you beginning to see that it isn't as we were taught? We don't become born again and then take the reins from God for our lives?

Because God knew and purposed both our good and bad that we do, then we can leave *everything* from the good part *and* the bad part in His hands as tools. Now, we have always been taught to put the good tools — the good things from the good part in God's hands — while 'protecting God' by holding the bad tools or bad things from the bad part in our hands. How little we learn and grow by thinking we must protect God's image!

Look at some bad tools God used to get Moses where he was to be in God's plan: the leader of a nation of newly freed slaves!

God used these bad things to get Moses —

1. **Born**: that cost a lot of male babies both killed and in peril for Moses to come into Pharaoh's very home to be raised with the best education in the world — to learn leadership from the greatest living leader.

2. **Into the desert** in order to become a nobody. That cost the death of an Egyptian overseer, bringing Moses' fear of the royal family.

3. **Into Jethro's life and tent**. That cost the bullying of Jethro's daughters.

4. **Out of Egypt with the Hebrews**. That cost Pharaoh hardening his own heart and God then hardening it completely. That cost the death of an entire Egyptian army and so many, many firstborn children and animals! WHY? So God could use Pharaoh to show the Israelites His Glory.

Did You Like the Movie?

God knows His plan. He cannot, He will not manipulate because He *is* integrity. What you may see as God's failure contingency was figured in before the Garden grew grass. God has already been 'everywhere' in time. He knew each of our specific plans because of His great love for us.

"God's plan for the world stands up, all His designs are made to last."[82] Again, "the plans of the LORD stand firm forever, the purposes of His heart through all generations."[83] He promised an unshakable plan, solid as a rock. It is as unchangeable as His love.

How can I best explain this? Consider the making of a movie. A writer writes a script. A producer raises financing. A director casts people that he chooses for parts that were written for them. The director manipulates each aspect of the production to bring about what the writer envisioned and the audience watches. Actors make choices, but only within the director's / producer's / writer's designs. Actors do not write, direct, film, do make-up, supply special effects, orchestrate stunts, carry out the logistics for the movie company or edit and market the film. We *see* the actors throughout. We *see and think* they are important, I mean, look at the screen! See the actors?

But actors are very, very limited. An actor plays a small part in the overall movie, and again, his part is completely orchestrated. So is your role in the movie *Planet Earth*.

For eons men and religions blamed Adam and Eve for their part in a creative, thoughtful, beautiful movie. Title the movie *Plan of Love,* or *Plan of Redemption,* or maybe even *Plan of Hope.* Look at us, you and me, actors in a script. What choices did we have in assuming our roles? None! Did we choose our parents, or where we were raised? Absolutely not! Did we choose the language our parents taught us? Did we choose the first schools

---

[82] Psalms 33:11 (MSG)
[83] Psalms 33:11 (NIV)

we attended as children? Did we choose how we would be raised in our formative years? Well? No!

Remember God's guarantee: He will complete the work He began. God guarantees no work that we begin.

Gentlemen, Start Your Engines

Have you ever heard the announcer at a car race say, "Gentlemen, start your engines!" It sounds like thunder erupts! You feel it in your chest! So, did you "start salvation's engine" in your life? Hardly. Think of this — when did His work in you first begin? How far before you came to Him did God begin His work in you? According to Romans, the eighth chapter, it was long before you thought about Him!

God began His plan in your genetics hundreds of generations ago. He began His work in your personality, both what was genetic and what was environmental from your infancy. God used teachers, aunts, uncles, siblings, and grandparents to pour into you. God provided resources — or knew which would be denied you. God similarly worked to provide your friends and mate long before you thought to need them! God provided witnesses to bring His Son to your family generations before you were born, or a witness to you apart from family and friends. God's plan was in motion and that brought you *to* Him. Reflect on your life.

I know you can recall experiences you had with Him, even before you were born again. I know I can and cherish them.

- ♥ Weren't there times you knew or felt like *someone* was watching out for you before you came to Him?
- ♥ Didn't He draw you repeatedly before you realized it and responded?
- ♥ Can you recall times when you could say, "Today, I would not have made it without *someone* watching over me?"
- ♥ Can you see God was there all along, watching, waiting, working and loving you?

Now, if God worked that far in advance for your *past*, who knows what He was doing for centuries for your life *tomorrow*? His will? Rest in Him, knowing that He is doing all that He promised to do in us, to bring us to our day when we bow before Jesus — complete, redeemed!

> And surely I am with you always, to the very end of the age
> — Jesus
> Matthew 28:20

So after God puts us where He wants us, after He puts in us what He destined, and after He equips us with all talents and gifts to carry out His plan, does He then leave us to accomplish it on our own? And in each success who gets the credit? Does God know the enemy's plots to delay our victories and derail our dreams? Are we on our own now? Never! No! Not with Him who loves us investing and guiding us, *even as we fight Him*!

All of us have failed but *none of us are failures;* it is impossible to fail when Christ's plan of love is in our lives. The day we were saved, He said to us, "Son, (daughter), I have a plan for your life and today I am going to start a work in you that I will continue until I bring you home." What hope and healing to you!

Now look at something I think you will find interesting, I know it is to me.

Good or Bad — God Provides

Adam & Eve did what God *told them not to do.* In time, their sons discovered God had provided animal sacrifices[84] and they were restored.

On the other hand, Abraham did exactly as God *told him to do* with Isaac. How achingly did Abraham travel to Moriah with his only son Isaac, thinking he would have to sacrifice his son's

---

[84] Genesis 4:4ff

life? How hard was it to labor up that mountain, obediently carrying everything for a sacrifice that would be his son? Again, God provided an animal sacrifice far more miraculously than for Adam's sons, but God provided in both situations. Could Adam take credit for covering his wife? Could Abraham claim credit for saving Isaac's life? Neither could! God's plan was already woven into their lives and was revealed to them, as it was unveiled throughout scripture like a tapestry!

God's plan in the Old Testament pointed to the New Testament and Jesus' blood shed for all of us whom He has chosen, sinner and saved alike. God's plan didn't wait on works to weave it or unveil it. Men played their roles, but they couldn't choose to limit God. When we blame parents, bosses, teachers or world events for bad things we forget, It's All About Him. When we take credit for good things, It's (still) All About Him. Good or bad, it's all in God's sovereign plan to complete us!

By the twitch of His little finger, in the twinkling of an eye, God could bring all the elect to Himself. He could save the whole world! Does He use preaching? Does He use our ministry gifts or anointed men of God? Yes! His Word says so! However He does not *need* them. He uses an infinite array of tools, those we think of as bad or good to bring about His Will.

You might ask if it is God's will that we all unlearn. I don't know what God's plan for your life is. Only He knows, so get to know Him better. I do think since you have read this book to this point that may indicate what God is up to in your life. Don't be anxious about it. He is at work in you, just as He promised.

GOD ASKS NONE OF US TO RESCUE HIS REPUTATION
WHEN THE WORLD EXPLODES

Surely I spoke of things I did not understand, things too wonderful for me to know. —Job

God has asked none of us to write His PR campaign. Jesus fulfilled God's script to reach Earth, played His role and died for us. Others have already written the toughest aspects of God's sovereignty but hear this believer's take on God's dominion.

Postcard From the Edge

Jeremiah walked woozily down demolished streets. His eyes stung. Once raging fires now smoldered, their acrid smoke burning his eyes. He got disoriented staring down paths in the wreckage through burned out hulks. He often thought he knew a street, but all its landmarks, every tree, every building was flattened. The crazy rubble made him wonder if he were even in what used to be a street.

That wasn't the worst of it.

Groans and whimpering wafted from the rubble. Some whimpered; guttural echoes ghosted from their homes or where buildings fell and burned them. Some retreated into ruins to die. Other echoes sounded frightening. Worse than the alien soldiers, whose breath and sweat stunk, and their strange laughter, curses, and cries, was the silence they left.

Where children had played, families had argued and laughed, lovers had whispered to each other was now only a silence of the dead, the defeated, and the dying. And the dying lay everywhere, so many dead. Dust and ash covered their corpses so they blended with piles of stone. The gaunt and burned ones smiled, showing teeth in eternal grins. Most corpses curled hideously disfigured by the soldiers' cruelty: children, mothers, old women, and the weak. He tired of shooing away vultures feeding, always feeding.

He had thrown up until his stomach was as empty as those of the sighing children with distended stomachs.

He had wept until he could cry no more. Now he was broken.

Jeremiah had told these people what was coming — for years. Sovereign Jehovah had renamed Jerusalem after prostitutes[85] who gave themselves as lovers to strange gods. Now their strange gods had come to town on foreign soldiers' shoulders.

Here is what Jeremiah wrote about God. Apart from his book of prophecy, these laments echo down his tear-stained streets as he mourns to God, to find something powerful. Here Jeremiah confronts God as He is. God delivered His promised judgment.

> **THE UNDETECTED SACREDNESS OF "CIRCUMSTANCES"**
>
> *All things work together for good to them that love God.*
> Romans 8:28
>
> God ordains the circumstances of a saint's life.
> In a saint's life there is no such thing as chance.
> God by His providence brings you into circumstances that you can never understand, but God's Spirit understands.
> —*Oswald Chambers*

Along with his country, Jeremiah had believed that God was first and foremost their protector. Confusion dogged his every stumbling step. If God were first and foremost a protector, He

---

[85] Jeremiah 31:11

wasn't as Jeremiah had thought. All before was in ruins, and now in its place Jeremiah found the truth.

God, "You Ripped Me to Pieces"

^{verse 5} He [God] hemmed me in, ganged up on me, [86]
poured on the trouble and hard times.
⁶ He locked me up in deep darkness,
like a corpse nailed inside a coffin.
⁷ He shuts me in so I'll never get out,
manacles my hands, shackles my feet.
⁸ Even when I cry out and plead for help,
He locks up my prayers and throws away the key.

¹⁰ He's a prowling bear tracking me down,
a lion in hiding ready to pounce.
¹¹ He knocked me from the path and ripped me to pieces.
When he finished, there was nothing left of me.
¹² He took out his bow and arrows
and used me for target practice.

¹⁴ Everyone took me for a joke,
made me the butt of their mocking ballads.

¹⁶ He ground my face into the gravel.
He pounded me into the mud.

¹⁷ I gave up on life altogether.
I've forgotten what the good life is like.
¹⁸ I said to myself, "This is it. I'm finished.
God is a lost cause."
¹⁹ I'll never forget the trouble, the utter lostness,
the taste of ashes, the poison I've swallowed.
²⁰ I remember it all—oh, how well I remember—
the feeling of hitting the bottom.

Oh, And I Remember One Other Thing, God

²¹ But there's one other thing I remember,
and remembering, I keep a grip on hope:
²² God's loyal love couldn't have run out,

---

[86] Lamentations 3:5-44 (MSG)

His merciful love couldn't have dried up.
²³ They're created new every morning.
How great your faithfulness!
²⁴ I'm sticking with God (I say it over and over).
He's all I've got left.
²⁵ God proves to be good to the man who passionately waits,
to the woman who diligently seeks.

So, What Do I Do With This Knowledge?

²⁶ It's a good thing to quietly hope,
quietly hope for help from God.
²⁷ It's a good thing when you're young
to stick it out through the hard times.
²⁸ When life is heavy and hard to take,
go off by yourself. Enter the silence.
²⁹ Bow in prayer.
Don't ask questions:
Wait for hope to appear.
³⁰ Don't run from trouble.
Take it full-face. The "worst" is never the worst.
³¹ Why?
Because the Master
won't ever walk out
and fail to return.
³² If He works severely,
He also works tenderly.
His stockpiles of loyal love
are immense.
³³ He takes no pleasure in making life hard,
in throwing roadblocks in the way:

³⁷ Who do you think "spoke and it happened"?
It's the Master who gives such orders.
³⁸ Doesn't the High God speak everything,
good things and hard things alike, into being?
⁴⁰ Let's take a good look at the way we're living and
reorder our lives under God.
⁴¹ Let's lift our hearts and hands,
praying to God in heaven:

God is bringing you
into places and
among people and
into conditions
so that the Spirit's
intercession
in you
may take a particular line.
Never put your hand
in front of the circumstances
to say,
"I am going to be
my own providence here.
I must watch this, and guard that."
All your circumstances
are in God's hand,
so never think it 'strange'
concerning *any*
of your circumstances.

Your part in intercessory
prayer
is not to enter into
the agony of intercession,
but to use the commonsense
circumstances God puts you in,
and the commonsense
people
He puts you amongst
by His providence,
to bring them
before God's throne and
give the Spirit in you
a chance to intercede for
them.
In this way God is going to
sweep the whole world with
His saints.

Oswald Chambers

It's hard to say, "I've had it worse than Jeremiah."

He preached Truth as a teen and was ridiculed. He was the most brilliant political analyst of his day, but was ignored until too late. He was beaten, arrested, ridiculed — and worse — proven right. Jerusalem was ravaged. Jeremiah's king watched all of his sons murdered before his eyes and then his eyes were put out so their deaths would be his last sight ever. Then he was marched to Babylon in chains. Jeremiah watched friends run to every country to die there. Those who remained died of disease, hunger, and horror.

Jeremiah pinned all of it where it belonged — on God.

And then he shocked us. After he pinned everything on God he asked the most daunting question of all — "What is truest about God?" This is what he weeps. This is what he writes.

His mercies are new every morning.

What is Jeremiah's bedrock when examining our Sovereign God?

The Master won't ever walk out and fail to return. If He works severely, He also works tenderly. His stockpiles of loyal love are immense.

What does Jeremiah trust utmost about God? Where does He come in life's storms?

God's loyal love couldn't have run out, His merciful love couldn't have dried up. [87]

Most who defend God make their defense here — in the middle of evil in our world. Interestingly, another who knew God talked of God's sovereignty in an entirely different place. You probably know this rogue as the apple of God's eye.

---

[87] Lamentations 3:22

How Else Do I Know That God is Sovereign?

David united Israel, became king and murdered, fornicated, chose adultery, lied, killed and he now was enraptured. Can you imagine? He was enraptured! Why was David overjoyed?

David found himself in the middle, unavoidably in the middle, of God's plan for his life. He was inextricably enmeshed in God's sovereign map for his life! God's plan of love for David had hurt him, brought him unimaginable loss, left him depressed and in a spiritual desert, and what does David say?

God, investigate my life; get all the facts firsthand. [88]
² I'm an open book to You; even from a distance,
    You know what I'm thinking.
³ You know when I leave and when I get back;
    I'm never out of Your sight.
⁴ You know everything I'm going to say
    before I start the first sentence.
⁵ I look behind me and You're there,
    then up ahead and You're there, too—
    Your reassuring presence, coming and going.
⁶ This is too much, too wonderful—
    I can't take it all in!
⁷ Is there anyplace I can go to avoid Your Spirit?
    to be out of your sight?
⁸ If I climb to the sky, You're there!
    If I go [to hell] underground, You're there!

    ¹² It's a fact: darkness isn't dark to You; night and day,
        darkness and light, they're all the same to You.
    ¹³ Oh yes, You shaped me first inside, then out;
        You formed me in my mother's womb.

---

[88] Psalms 139:1-13 (MSG) A David Psalm

David found himself in the place of a child who truly trusts his Father's love. Where else would a Father want His child, if not in the center of His love?

The Father wants His child in the middle of His love, to know God's purposes in her life. The Father has a plan for all of His daughters, for their good, for their joy and completion. Every earthly father of any stature takes the long view for his daughter. He sees her as possessing good opportunities. He sees her as beautiful, and sees himself as walking her down an aisle, wearing white and establishing her own home as an accomplished, beautiful, alive, and joyous woman.

Now, imagine this harrowing scene at your house.

As a dad (or mom) you have corrected your daughter. You then waited, hugged her, told her that you loved her, and she now asks if she can go out in the back yard and play. You smile and brush her hair back out of her face and then send her out to play.

You wash dishes for a few minutes, looking out the windows over the sink into the back yard when you realize that you can't see her. You can't see in back of the detached garage, so you figure she is back there, but something tugs at your heart, tugs at your parental instinct. It unsettles your stomach.

You dry your hands and walk out the back door and quietly descend the steps, listening and looking everywhere. For some reason you creep up to the corner of the garage and freeze when you hear your daughter around the corner saying, "Bad girl. You are terrible, a horrible girl. You are icky, and filthy and ugly!" and she whimpers. Your heart is breaking as you peer around the corner — and then your heart stops.

Your beautiful daughter is pricking herself with a safety pin, over and over on her perfect little forearm. You're sickened, hurt, questioning, angry and concerned all at the same time as you rush to her. She is confused that you are there, ashamed of what she is doing, and somehow still defying you.

Why does her behavior trouble you so? Why would your daughter be mutilating herself and why is that so troubling? Because as a parent, correcting your child, without breaking her spirit may be the most sacred aspect of parenting. Correcting a child and upholding her sense of your love is a precious if precarious balance.

Now here your child has taken what you thought was a completed correction — and she is going you one better. She is doing a more complete job of parenting herself by inflicting extra pain and shame from the pinpricks in her skin.

How like your daughter we are!

We dwell on pain and shame, repeatedly inflicting it by reliving horrible pieces of our lives. Unlike David, we are stuck in the sins of our youth. Unlike Jeremiah, we refuse to quit our lament and come to God's goodness.

In our shame we fear any lesson to be learned and we fear God. And God? He is horrified to see us take over His job as corrector and Parent to us.

At the opposite end of self-mutilation, which is coincidentally increasing in our children, we see others of us who react to God's plan, to His direction for our lives with apathy.

If God as our Father uses all to our good, which He promised, how can apathy even occur without His allowing it and using it for our good? Through John, God warns of apathy, using a term *lukewarm*.[89] *Chliaros* means tepid. This person is no great sinner, but no great saint. Not anything: apathetic. God spews that person from His mouth, the only truly frightening possibility among all those we have discussed.

But even in apathy, how can there ever be anything that happens to a child of God
- ♥ Without God doing it or
- ♥ Without God allowing Satan to do it (as in Job's case)?

---

[89] Revelation 3:16

Either way, it will be used for His child's good or He never would allow it to happen!

Any event in God's hands transforms so many areas of our lives! My pastor, David Willets, emphasizes God's kindness and sovereignty when our world explodes — and God is shaping us.

Around noon on Thursday, March 4, 2004, I leaned into the car to kiss goodbye my wife, Leesa, and daughter, Lauryn, as they drove away to Oklahoma from our home in Ruston, Louisiana. Leesa and I shared 27 rich years of life. Beautiful, energetic Lauryn was looking at Oklahoma Baptist University for school in the fall. They drove away and I breathed in the spring azaleas and jasmine and returned to a busy day.

I received a mid afternoon trip update as Leesa talked over their music and laughter on her cell phone. After a few minutes Leesa said, "I need to get off the phone. It's starting to rain." We expressed our love to each other and hung up. They were nearing the end of their seven-hour trip to Tulsa, traveling on the Indian Nation's Turnpike that they had driven before.

It was unusual for me not to have heard from the girls by seven. As I sat on the deck of our house with the sun slowly vanishing, something caught my eye in the house: a flashlight beaming through the front door. I walked through the house and opened the door to two Louisiana State Troopers.

As a pastor, I had faced this situation before. I thought, "Someone in the church is in trouble and they need my help." What one of the troopers said shook my life to its foundation: "Dr. Willets, there has been an accident on the Indian Nation's Turnpike in Oklahoma." He handed me a Teletype:

> AT 4:05P.M. THERE WAS A VEHICLE ACCIDENT ON THE INDIAN NATION'S TURNPIKE AT HIGHWAY MARKER 69 NEAR MCALESTER. TWO FATALITIES: LEESA WILLETS AND LAURYN WILLETS OF RUSTON, LOUISIANA.

Reeling, all I could say was, "They are dead? Wait. They are dead?"

When the Holy Spirit inspired the apostle Paul to write: "We know that in all things God works for the good of those who love Him, who have been called according to His purpose"[90] — God had long ago planned this "accident" in my life for His purpose. It was His sovereign plan and will. He would prove faithful to His Word.

There is nothing "good" about your wife and daughter being killed in a car wreck. But God's Word does not say 'everything will be good.' It says, *"We know that in all things God **works for the good**."* It would take another book to account the ways this event has impacted my life and the lives of thousands, but let me share highlights of how God has worked for the good for me.

*My theology grew up. I used to explain a world-exploding event like this: "What a horrible effect of living in a fallen world! Death is part of a fallen world. This is not what God originally intended, but man

> When we are praying about the result, say, of a battle or a medical consultation the thought will often cross our minds that (if only we knew it) the event is already decided one way or the other.
>
> I believe this to be no good reason for ceasing our prayers. The event certainly has been decided. In a sense it was decided 'before all worlds.' But one of the things taken into account in deciding it, and so one of the things that really cause it to happen, may be this very prayer that we are now offering. Thus, shocking as it may sound, I conclude that we can at noon become part causes of an event occurring at ten a.m. (Some scientists would find this easier than popular thought does.)
> C.S. Lewis

---

[90] Romans 8:28 (NIV)

made the choice to bring sin into our world, and sin brings death to us all. God now comforts those who grieve with a hope to see our loved ones who know Christ as Savior in heaven."

But this dark night of my soul drove me to read Scripture with renewed eyes. Now I know: "God is infinitely Sovereign. Nothing happens by 'accident.' His plan directs or allows every event in our lives to draw us closer to Him, to make us more like Him. He loves us that much. Glory to His name!"

*Life is now prioritized. God planted a passion to aid anyone who desires to be Jesus Christ's true disciple, not people who can profit me in some way. No other cause, no matter how "churchy" it appears, ignites my interest. I clearly see how this event had to happen for these priorities to take shape.

*God brought me a new wife in the most wonderful way. No coincidence, see God's sovereignty at work. The Kilpatrick family owns several funeral homes and they served in the church I pastored. A life-long member of that church, Melanie, also served at their funeral home in Ruston. God's detailed hand placed Melanie to direct Leesa and Lauryn's funerals. Much later, in His time, God brought us together as husband and wife.

*Through shared pain, my son, Landon, and I have become best friends. No, the girls' death did not have to happen for us to reach this level of friendship. However, God planned that this event would bring us closer than we would have ever been.

*God opened a door for a new ministry: a church with no properties or borders in Tulsa now allows me to pursue my prioritized passions: www.numachurch.com.

*I know God is our unshakable Rock in the worst storms. Yes, I sank in pain and anguish after the girls' deaths. It was so crushing that I thought I would despair, but God revealed that side of His nature, which I had only glimpsed before — although I had preached on it many times. One evening three weeks after their passing, I entered 'our' house again — greeted by deathly silence. No more laughter from Lauryn and warmth of Leesa would greet me here. I shuffled to my bedroom and collapsed on the floor weeping uncontrollably. From the depth of my soul I cried to God, "You have put too much on me this time! This is more than I can bear! If You don't come to me in some way, I will despair!"

At that point, I didn't know what to expect.

Would God come to me as the *paraklesis* (comforter, consoler)? He did not.

Would He come to me as *Abba* (daddy, papa)? He did not.

I felt no warm fuzzy feelings. God came as the Great "I Am." As a tall granite mountain, God spoke to my spirit, "Son, I know you are sinking, but I will not be moved." At that, God stopped my free-fall downward and set my soul on solid ground.

I now fear nothing. My God will not be moved by any circumstances of life. He is my solid Rock on which I stand. In Job's words, my belief in God's sovereignty extends to this declaration, *"Though he slay me, yet will I trust in him."* [91]

Wow. God gently, surely showed David His plan even as it seemed that David's world exploded. I was amazed at all the different areas of David's life God shaped when David saw God as sovereign in "the accident" Often, we are beset by much smaller trials that grow to test our hearts and prove God's goodness. Do we hunt God's goodness as we walk through these smaller events?

I earned a speeding ticket here in Tulsa a couple of years ago. I later bought a new car and asked for my new son-in-law to insure the cars, leaving my agent of many years. Our first insurance premium with this new company was $7,500 per year. I didn't think much of it as my wife had also bought a new car. Then the new company found that two-year-old speeding ticket and one on my wife's records, and increased the premium another $800 per year. I either needed a heart surgeon or to check it out. I realized my old company would not access that penalty, so I contacted my

---

[91] Job 13:15

old agent to find that he would continue my insurance, and add my wife's car for a total premium $3,000 under the new company. WOW. Had my ticket not been added, I never would have checked back with my old agent! The ticket (and I hated getting it) saved me $3,000 per year. Do you look for His goodness in back of the trauma, no matter what size it is?

Traditional Schools Defend God

Most of us have no formal ministerial training. Fortunately, we have many who do. Unfortunately, if we throw things at them that go against their trained belief system, they invoke the fact that we have no training. Lawyers are the same. What they learn in law school is the way to solve problems, and as a rule, they don't ever think of them in a different way.

I find that lawyers and ministers who fall back on their training also often fail to think outside the box, much less climb out of the box with a new thought. As I have wrestled with this message and ministerial friends, they often follow steps that are starting to feel predictable.

Ministers come to a point of acknowledgement.

- ♥ They may border on agreement.
- ♥ They find, however, that unless they entertain what goes against their belief system (learned in sacred *ministerial training*)
- ♥ They cannot find more truth and grow.

What is also predictable in talking of God's sovereignty is that as a minister discusses God's rule —

- ♥ He is prone to make it sound like it's all about him (or her). He *begins* discussing God's sovereignty, but ends up talking about himself and his freedom or his will or the ramifications of God's sovereignty on him rather than focus on God.

So this teaching that everything focuses on God or His sovereign plan for us is of God or of Satan. It can't be both. It can't be *neither*.

If it isn't of God, then I am spiritually so far off base and so immature that I can't even sense Satan using me.

You say, "Scary."

But if that's the case, I wouldn't call that scary either. I still see God working in me as He promised He would. For what? For His good purpose.

For how long?

Until it is completed, until He redeems me, until He brings me home.

Just how beautiful is that?

I trust God more than anything I have written in this or in my first book. To me, it doesn't get more beautiful than God. God, who made white-capped mountains, stunning sienna sunsets, white and azure beaches, is beautiful. Painfully beautiful. And He is making me — into His image. Beautiful.

He is beautiful, and I trust His beauty being formed in me more than everything else I see in me, or in the world around me.

7

GOD ASKS NONE OF US TO RESCUE HIS REPUTATION *WHEN HE WORKS IN SOMEONE*

Again, I trust God more than anything I have written in this or in my first book. To me, all beauty comes from God's beauty. He Who made blue glaciers, stunning corrals, shimmering stars, and thundering waterfalls is beautiful. Painfully beautiful. And He is making me into His image.

He is beautiful, and I trust His beauty being formed in me more than everything else I see in me, or in the world around me.

On the other hand, religion continually drums into us, that in and of ourselves we are bad. Constantly we hear that when we sin, which we have done / do / will do, we are *so* unrighteous. And we are unrighteous, within ourselves. Our works are unrighteous,

filthy rags;[92]

ugly in comparison to God's righteousness —

super weak rags in our own strength

Until I see my sin as God sees it and He sees each of His children as righteous! God calls us righteous because of what He has done for us. Period. Write it down. He sees us this way —
> Blessed are you, whose transgressions are forgiven,
> whose sins are covered.
> Blessed are you whose sin the LORD does not count against you.[93]
> In the gospel a righteousness from God is revealed,
> a righteousness that is by faith from first to last. [94]

---
[92] Isaiah 64:6
[93] Psalm 32:1-2

> To you who do not work
> *but trust God*
> Who justifies the wicked,
> Your faith is credited as righteousness. [95]

Regardless. Regardless of how we see it. Regardless of how we feel. We are righteous because of Christ and His cleansing from the Cross. God said so. It's true because He is true.

But God says that He points out our sin (convicts us) so that we will see it and confess it. What happens when we confess it? This is what God says. "If we admit our sins—make a clean breast of them — He won't let us down; *He'll be true to Himself.* He'll forgive our sins and purge us of all wrongdoing."[96]

What does God do? "He'll be true to Himself. He'll forgive our sins and purge us of all wrongdoing." [97]

What does religion nailed to poor theology do? It creates fear and guilt. Stuck in fear and guilt we accomplish little for God. In fear we risk less. In guilt we love less. Now what does our sin nailed to the cross accomplish? Forgiven, we are free of shame and guilt. Say it: "Free of guilt." Say it: "Free of shame."

Say it.

Hear yourself say it.

"Forgiven, I (Your name), am free of guilt and shame!"

We will only see this when we are willing

to see our sin,

to see us as God sees our sin and

God sees us apart from our sin.

As long as we see our sin and ourselves as man and religion sees us, we will live in guilt and shame's filth and squalor! Are you not tired of the rundown tenement of guilt and shame?

---

[94] Romans 1:17
[95] Romans 4:5-6
[96] 1 John 1:9 (MSG)
[97] 1 John 1:9

This is why God tells us to study the Word, to "proclaim the Message with intensity; keep on your watch. Don't ever quit. *Just keep it simple.*" [98]

When we see what the Book says, we learn how wrong poor theology and poor religion are.

We learn who we really are in God's providence, His care and plan for us.

We learn that especially in our dark spots God placed a desire in us to study His Book, to *see* Him in its pages and to outgrow our limited theology.

We learn, how to "keep our way pure — by living according to Your Word!"[99]

Again, "I have hidden Your word in my heart that I might not sin against you."[100] And how does God's Word paint His sovereignty? "I am sure that God Who began the good work within you will keep right on helping you grow in His grace until His task within you is finally finished on that day when Jesus Christ returns." [101]

All of the same comfortable answers and same well-worn sermons leave us feeling that God's response to sin is — uncertain. Think about it. Religionists hedge their bets when they preach. Look how they hedge their bets and see my questions —

> ➢ BUT we *keep on* sinning. *That surprises God?*
> **Emphasis on Him or us?**
>
> ➢ BUT our sin is *so* terrible. *God doesn't know us?*
> **Emphasis on Him or us?**
>
> ➢ BUT *He is* also just, jealous, righteous, and wrathful.
> **Emphasis on what is *truest* about God?**

Religionists preach God as if He is Jekyll and Hyde. How can we be sure of Who receives us as sinners? How do we know

---

[98] 2 Timothy 4:2 (MSG)
[99] Psalm 119:9
[100] Psalm 119:11
[101] Philip. 1:6

that *this quality* (His loving plan) and not *those others* (jealous, wrathful) are *most true* about God, the Father?

How do we KNOW what is truest about God, Jehovah?

The Bible tells us, that when God wanted to show us His truest self, He showed us Jesus. And the Book says this about Jesus as a picture of God, "Jesus Christ is the same yesterday and today and forever."[102] We trust God's unchanging character as Protector and Provider, even if we are where He is working out tough things in us. We can trust what Jesus showed was truest about God, is still truest about Him today.

What was truest about God was, is, and ever will be Jesus. What is truest today, no matter what today holds, is Jesus.

Sidetracks and Derailments

I had invited Joe to my home. [103] He came over one evening to play a motivational film chock full of New Age garbage. We finished watching, and standing, pacing and watching my face, he was obviously excited, until he saw my reaction.

I said, "You know, Joe you studied at our nationally recognized Christian college here. You've been ordained as a minister. And by your excitement, it's obvious that you are drawn to this film's dictates. In one way, I am excited about that and in another, I'm sad."

His face contorted, he could not settle on a half-smile or shock. He fidgeted.

"Joe, if you choose to go with this, as I think you will because something in you wants what's in the film more than you want what Christ desires for your life. Let me say that again, something in you wants YOU to be more like what is in the film than to be like Christ. I am sad for the pain it will cause you and how much it will cost you to learn what Christ is truly like in God's Word.

---

[102] Hebrews 13:8
[103] Not his name, of course.

But Joe, I'm excited for the beauty of this. God will use this to do a work in you. Why? Because He loves you. Why? Because He began His work in you, and He is continuing it in you, just as He is in me and all His children."

Joe now slid down into a chair. His face was cloudy.

I continued, "Joe, What a freedom it brings when we see that God is at work in us. And, oh, you can trust Him. Totally, you can trust Him even, especially as you head in rebellion's direction. Why? Because He made you, all that you are, and now He spends the rest of your life working the not-like-Christ-parts out of you to make you more like Him. How beautiful is that? It's all about Him, about His plan for you. Its all about His love for you, Joe."

He was staring at me by now. His jaw had passed his chest, bounced off his lap, and was on the floor.

"Joe, God looks at you and says, 'Son, I knew before creating earth, or saving you, I knew the direction you hoped to take now. Just as I did in Adam and Eve's case, I knew your heart's choice today. Still, I love you and yes, even this is part of My workmanship in you to make you more like Me."

He was shocked. He now sat quietly, looking at his hands. He looked torn. How often do we all feel so torn? God shines His light on us to illuminate our chosen direction today as dark and wrong, not at all like Christ and it breaks our hearts!

He finally stammered, "But that would make me a robot!"

I replied, "So? Would it bother you if you were God's robot? What better calling could we have than to be our Lord's robot?"

He surged back to say, "I could tweak this to use it. It would be powerful!"

I said. "Joe, you won't be the first or the last one to think he could play in Satan's sand box and win. But the good news is, again, God will use even this to make you more like Him. And Joe —"

He almost mouthed it with me, "Isn't that beautiful?"

If every way that you express your "freedom" is destructive, why wouldn't you hope to be "less free"? Being robotic but obedient rather than destructively free seems attractive, to say the least.

So I have come to the wild point of God's sovereignty.

This book says,

SATAN: GOD'S DESIGNED

No accident. Adam and Eve didn't surprise God. God designed this —

TOOL
For God to intentionally use to grow His children.

This drives those who teach that sin caught God 'off guard' crazy.

It flies in the face of those who say God works against sin in the world so He can help us survive here.

To even give it thought enrages many. Their reactions mean this is powerful. Their reactions show this touches something in us causing us to react out of fear. We fear entertaining something we don't know and have believed its opposite since childhood. Change ushers in fear when the change involves going against long-held beliefs. What a paradox! We know we're short on answers, but at the same time we won't risk changing answers. How scary!

A great little book to explore the beauty in risking to see change is titled *Who Moved My Cheese*. Get it. Read it. You will grow.

God didn't apologize to Paul. God changed him.

Paul experienced God on a road near Damascus.

God gave Paul a vision of Himself, and asked Paul why He was persecuting Jesus.

It almost did Paul in, just as it has us at times and will continue to do us in until we are complete before God. It did blind him.

God sent a man named Ananias to give back Paul's vision, both his spiritual and his physical seeing. [104]

And then God began to explain to Paul, "I picked [you] as my personal representative to Gentiles, kings and Jews. And I'm about to show [you] what [you're] in for—the hard suffering that goes with this job."[105]

God sent Paul very clear and emphatic directions for him. He would suffer. Our Lord said in effect, "I will overmaster your whole life. You will have no end, no aim, and no purpose but Mine."

Why?

"I chose you. You will be My bond slave." How far above 'robot' would you rate that? Not far, I am sure.

God then gives Paul no *given message*, or *doctrine* to proclaim. No, God brought Paul into a vivid, personal, overmastering relationship to Jesus Christ — as Lord. As Sovereign. As Master.

God made Paul "an instrument I chose." And then God called Paul.

Think of it another way. We often answer the question "What is God's will for my life?"

    with circumstances,

    with things,

    with fleeting material stuff!

---

[104] Acts 9:11
[105] Acts 9:15-16 (MSG)

I "want" to live in *this* house, I "need" to be driving *this* car, I "should" meet with success in this deal, and I "have to have" these people as friends. I "need" these things to give me comfort. I "want" this circumstance to make me happy. We would never say it, but we are tempted to *live* saying: "God, how I want control of my life! How I want what I want. I will even use prayer to beg for it!" Again, we would never say those things aloud, but they are equally dangerous, unstated and secure in our hearts.

Things are not necessarily God's will, only when they come after first seeking God's Kingdom.[106] Possessions and circumstances may be unimportant to Him unless they produce something amazing — *you*.

God's will for Paul's life *was Paul*: missionary to Europe, civilized people, literate people, you and me. God's will for Paul *was the Apostle Paul* we know and love. What had Paul done correctly up to that point? I can easily argue that he had done nothing good, but God stopped him cold in the road. How? God's love and grace fell on Paul! God continued His process begun in Paul before Paul fell on his face before Jesus. God changed Paul's circumstances to change the man, to begin conforming Paul to be like Christ.

God's purpose was a man named Paul — and all events would flow around Paul to build him as God's child! Some of Paul's circumstances were happy: some were not. What did Paul write about that? "Actually, I don't have a sense of needing anything personally. I've learned[*] by now to be quite content whatever my circumstances. I'm just as happy with little as with much, with much as with little. I've found the recipe for being happy whether full or hungry, hands full or hands empty." [107] What did it mean to Paul to be quite content as a believer?

---

[106] Matthew 6:33
[*] Personally, I am learning more and more all the time on this one!
[107] Philip. 4:11-12

"Whatever I have, wherever I am, I can make it through anything in the One who makes me who I am." [108]

How does it translate into us? Do we pray for circumstances or the reality, "Lord, I want to know You and I am utterly thankful to be Your child?" I used to say what I heard others say, "I have had money and I haven't, and I know which I like best." Today I say, "I know which I like best and it is Him, money or no money."

- ♥ God isn't making our car into anything. It will burn at the end of the world.
- ♥ He isn't making our wardrobe into anything lasting (even to next year!)
- ♥ God isn't creating a country club membership as something eternal.
- ♥ He isn't converting your three-bedroom condo into anything in heaven.

These are temporary tools, but only as they aid in shaping an eternal reality — who *you* are in Christ. What am I saying? God makes *us* into His will. Yes, He does. And in focusing on Him in us, we see it in everything we read and hear of God's great salvation story.

Listen to God talk about His first Child, Jesus. God set Jesus as our model for living in these lines from the first Christian praise chorus. This hymn does not focus on Christ's circumstances, but on the reality of Who Christ was and is.

Let the same mind be in you
That was in Christ Jesus,
Who, though He was in the form of God,
did not regard equality with God
as something to be exploited,
but emptied Himself,
taking the form of a slave,
being born in human likeness.

---

[108] Philip. 4:13

> And being found in human form,
> He humbled Himself and
> became obedient to the point of death
> even death on a cross.
> Therefore God also highly exalted Him and
> gave Him the name that is above every name,
> so that at the name of Jesus
> every knee should bend,
> in heaven and on earth and under the earth,
> and every tongue should confess that
> "Jesus Christ is Lord,"
> to the glory of God the Father. [109]

We see God's truth in this early Christian hymn. As they sang of Jesus, they sang, "every tongue will confess that 'Jesus Christ is Lord,'" that it happened "to the glory of God the Father." Their song moved back in time to creation, and then forward to the cross, where Jesus showed God's glory. Moving through time to the climactic hour when every tongue will confess Christ's Kingship — to God's glory. That, especially, is to God's glory! All knees will then bow to Him and declare, "It's *All* About God."

Wrong Title. Backwards Emphasis.

I repeat: we preach that it is all about us, when It's All about Him. See another example. I see titles to sermons from preachers I respect.

> *End of Story! Prodigal gets the party!*
>
> *Prodigal's Homecoming!*

This parable is preached about a Prodigal Son when it is about God's grace! I love this story of God's grace and love. It

---

[109] Philippians 2:5-11 (NRSV)

plays to the heart of this book, but the hero of the story is not the silly son. The protagonist is not the impatient, impenitent son. The hero is the Loving Father. The parable trumpets God's persistence, not our depravity.

Let's carefully back up in Jesus' day to see the *three* stories He told together about His Father's unbounded, irrefutable, unstoppable love.

STORY 1 —Jesus told a story of a shepherd who had ninety-nine sheep safe in the fold, but he was a *shepherd*, not some hireling. He was the real deal. This shepherd was like God the Father as our Shepherd.[110] So what did he do? He left ninety-nine sheep and went hunting, risking everything to find that one sheep. Why? He wasn't a shepherd for all one hundred sheep while one was lost. The story is about the lost sheep? No. The story is about the Good Shepherd.

STORY 2 — Jesus switched quickly to a woman who had ten silver coins and lost one.[111] What did she do? She lit lamps, swept her dirt floor down on her hands and knees in every room until she found that coin. Then she told all her neighbors at 10 p.m.! Is the story about a lost coin? Get serious. It's about the woman who would not give up on her tenth coin until she had all of them back in her piggy bank.

STORY 3 — Now Jesus shifted to our larger story — but with the same theme. Just as in the other two parables Jesus characterized the real-deal shepherd and a woman who would not give up on what was hers, so He now characterized the Loving Father in a story that has since been told in thousands of books and movies with homecomings that still tug on our heart strings. Look at the story carefully.

- ♥ The Loving Father gives the younger son what he wants, knowing it will ruin him.[112]

---

[110] Luke 15:3
[111] Luke 15:8
[112] Luke 15:11

- ♥ The Loving Father lives with a joyless older son waiting, waiting every day. The older, obedient son got to live large, eat large and wear the finest clothes, a large life with a father he didn't know![113]
- ♥ The Loving Father spots his prodigal long before he gets home.[114]
- ♥ Not waiting for the boy, he runs to meet his broken son.[115]
- ♥ He brushes aside the boy's rehearsed speech[116] that he is a loser.[117]
- ♥ The Father knew his son has learned from pigs. He restores his credit and family status. [118]
- ♥ The Loving Father calls for the party, and why?
- ♥ The story tells how the Father reacted to his son who woke up and returned to him. [119]
- ♥ The Father doesn't apologize and even chides the older son because it was his responsibility to call for parties all these years as the owner of the estate![120]

Jesus was telling us again, "It's All About Dad." The stories of God's Bible center on His undeniable plan for the lives of His beloved, His children.

God does not need us to plan His PR campaign when He is working in one of His children.

---

[113] Luke 15:31
[114] Luke 15:20
[115] Luke 15:20
[116] Luke 15:21
[117] Luke 15:22
[118] Luke 15:22
[119] Luke 15:24
[120] When the Father probated his will to give the younger son what was 'due him', he had to give the older son his two thirds that belonged to him, obviously giving him the estate since they all still lived there.

8

GOD ASKS NONE OF US TO RESCUE HIS REPUTATION *WHEN IT FEELS PERSONAL.*

We have looked at God's Sovereignty when it feels like the world is exploding all around us, and when we know He is working in us. Face it. Those may not be the scariest or hardest times for us to experience God's loving Plan for our lives. It may be hardest when the rest of the world seems fine, and only our little part of it seems to be imploding — when everything happening feels personal. The Bible clearly tells the tale of how that feels in one man's story.

God never apologized to Job.

Job's story is about God's sovereignty, but where is that preached? Preachers sidestep God's sovereignty by stressing that —

Job stayed in agreement with God;
Job stayed faithful even after his wife cursed him, and
Job trusted God in spite of his friends.

Then, God restored all that was lost — translated — it's all about Job! That's like telling a story of terrible stepsisters, a horrid stepmother, pumpkin coaches and a heartbroken prince, and apologetically mumbling something about "Cinderella" as you finish.

Give Job his due, God made him amazing for His purposes, but Job's story is about God, and it is about God when He seems hardest to trust. Never lose sight of this: God created Job, just as he was. God was growing Job and using him for His plan. God seems hard to trust when everything we fear is happening, and God more than knows — He is pushing the agenda and the agenda feels personal! Look at the story.

God starts the ball rolling. Do you remember traveling in the car with your brothers or sisters? Do you remember what happened? Fights started in the back seat — with a look; maybe a face or your stupid sibling crossed the invisible line into your space with a finger. Worst of all, he started *touching* you. Things erupted into a fight, and your mother turned to say, "Stop that!"

And in unison, you both said, "He/She started it!"

Have no doubt. God started it. God pointed out Job to Satan. "Have you considered my servant Job? There is no one on earth like him; he is blameless and upright, a man who fears God and shuns evil." [121]

It gets harder to defend God. God gives Satan permission to take Job's wealth, house and Job's ten children![122]

It gets still harder to defend God: God gives Satan permission to attack Job's body.[123]

At this point Job's three buddies hear of his affliction. They come to him. At first, they're shocked. Job is unrecognizable. They then do something so amazing, so perceptive, and so sensitive: they sit silently for a week mourning with him. What great friends![124] Then they do something predictable: they start doing theology. Don't you hate it when you need someone to minister to you or console you and he or she does theology for you? Job's friends only had one song to sing, theologically speaking —

"God only punishes bad people, Job.

---

[121] Job 1:8
[122] Job 1:12
[123] Job 2:6
[124] Job 2:13

> *Confess now, buddy.*
> *What did you do wrong?*
> *What did you do so wrong that only God knows*
> *and He's punishing you?"*[125]

Job only had one response, over and over. "I don't get it. I didn't do anything to deserve this. I trust God though He seems distant and not trustworthy today."

Job had two other visitors: one small, and one great. The small visitor is a pup among old dogs, a young man named Elihu. He waits for the three older guys to wail on Job, and Job to rebuff them. The first time we see Elihu, he was "very angry with Job for justifying himself rather than God."[126]

Then he asks a question so he can answer it —
Why complain that God answers none of your questions? [127]

> God does speak —
> now one way, now another —
> even when we miss it. [128]
> In a dream,
> in a vision of the night. [129]
> He can speak in my ears,
> or terrify me with warnings. [130]
> He may chasten me on a bed of pain.[131]
> Food may become repulsive.[132]
> My flesh may waste away.[133]
> He passes me near messengers of death. [134]
> I may pray and find favor with Him.
> I may see God's face and shout for joy.

---

[125] Eliphaz, Bildad, and Tophar repeat these in speeches repeatedly for 29 chapters with Job's response.
[126] Job 32:2
[127] Job 33:13
[128] Job 33:14
[129] Job 33:15
[130] Job 33:16
[131] Job 33:19
[132] Job 33:20
[133] Job 33:21
[134] Job 33:22

> God might restore me to His righteous state.[135]
> God does all these things to a man —
> twice, even three times —
> to turn back his soul from the pit,
> that the light of life may shine on him. [136]

Then Elihu shows God's sovereignty in a simple way that both the redeemed and the lost take for granted: "If God withdrew His spirit and breath, all mankind would perish together." [137] No part of our existence exists apart from God.

And further, Elihu sings out what the whole Bible says of God's sovereignty for the righteous, "God is mighty and firm in His purpose. He never takes His eyes off the righteous to exalt them forever." [138] Elihu says that God has a purpose, even when we feel that His protection has been removed — especially when everything seems personal!

Why does God's favor and protection seemingly come and go, then? This young guy has a simple, audacious answer. God is always moving in ONE direction, to bring us into God's plan for perfecting us. Don't take my word for it. Read his words.

> God is wooing you
> from the jaws of distress
> to a spacious place
> free from restriction,
> to the comfort of your table
> laden with choice food.
> But now you're laden
> with judgments due the wicked.
> Neither your wealth nor
> all your mighty efforts
> can sustain you so that you escape distress? [139]

---

[135] Job 33:26
[136] Job 33:29-30
[137] Job 34:14-15
[138] Job 36:5-7
[139] Job 36:16-19

Elihu also warns us not to "base our case" on our own efforts, our thoughts, or our actions. As a lawyer, this seized my attention: "We cannot draw up our case before Him because of our darkness." [140] We are stuck in our thinking, trapped in our darkness, thinking, "God is beyond our understanding!" [141] Hear Elihu's trust. Remember Job's house is smoldering. Job's wife is squawking. Sitting in ashes, Job is using potsherds to scrape pustules from his skin. Elihu says, "God's voice thunders in marvelous ways. He does great things beyond our understanding."[142] And Elihu ends with this tribute to God's sovereignty.

> The Almighty is beyond our reach.
> Exalted in power.
> Just.
> Greatly righteous.
> So we revere Him,
> for does He not have regard
> for all the wise in heart?"

How many times have I said we must unlearn our religious, binding thinking? God condemns Job's three friends' theology, but condemns nothing from Elihu. Job's friends' religiosity offended God. "My servant Job will pray for you, and I will accept his prayer and not deal with you according to your folly. You have not spoken of Me what is right, as my servant Job has." [143]

Job told his friends, "This is all about God." Day after day, argument after argument, he simply told them, "This is all about God. I don't 'get it'. I wish He owed me an answer, but this is all about God."

Elihu agreed with Job.

So did God.

---

[140] Job 37:19
[141] Job 36:26
[142] Job 37:5
[143] Job 42:7-8

Job made sacrifices for his three friends and prayed for them. God forgave them.

What silly, binding, "it's all about me" theology are you still harboring?

Take the Credit. Don't take the credit.

We use many phrases to take credit for what happens in our lives. We "surrender", we "give"; and we speak of "our obedience."

We then wrap up our efforts by "giving all the credit to God."

Give yourself a simple test.

Get a tape or digital recorder. Talk about something that God has done in your life. Talk about your salvation experience, your sense of calling, using the gifts God gave you, how you went through yesterday. Record yourself. Then count pronouns. How many pronouns are first person: I, me, my, mine, myself, our, we, us. Now count the number of third person pronouns (Him, His, God) or second person pronouns (You, Your if you are talking as if to God) that apply to God.

How many pronouns are "about you"? _____

How many pronouns are "about God"? _____

Most often we are the heroes of our own stories. We are the focus, we grow, we give, we learn, we overcome, and we mention God at the end, as if tossing a bone to a dog. Or think of it this way: we are the box and present inside, and even the wrapping paper. God is just the bow that makes it so pretty. How sad.

When we fall prey to God as wrapping only, we open ourselves up to deception. If you've seen the documentary, *The Secret*, that I mentioned earlier you saw at the end of the film that they made it appear to be a spiritual presentation by wrapping it in god-like comments. That's like beautifully gift-wrapping a box of poisonous snakes. When we reduce God to wrapping and bows, then others can deceive us by beautifully gift-wrapping lies.

All of our testimony must focus on HIM. And only when we see His all in us, and that we are nothing more than His instruments, do we see the deep truth of our lives. Only as He plays us as His instruments do we join in a chorus thundering through galaxies to His glory will we take our place, our created, our beautiful place in creation.

He created us for this purpose — to live and breathe His glory.

Think of it. If that is so, did He then leave it up to us to make everything happen? NO!!

God left it up to Himself. He is our beginning and our finish. He is the best of what we are and what He wants us to be. We can't know our future starting in an hour. That being true, how could God create us for His purpose and then leave our lives up to us? He wouldn't. He hasn't.

It's All About Him. And yes, God who bothered to number the hairs on our head[144] is truly involved in every aspect of our lives. Robot? Does that bother you? If it does, be ready to be bothered, because that is the way it is.

Most of our testimonies are not about God. They are about us. Most sermons are not about God. They focus on us. Here is where it gets interesting. As we fail to praise how God works in us because we are praising ourselves, then we fail to see what to give Him the credit for doing. We also fail to see how He used other people in our lives.

> ➢ We take credit for learning what we actually heard on the radio, and claim it as our own insight.
> ➢ We take credit for doing what our parents modeled for us a thousand times.

---

[144] Matthew 10:30, Luke 12:7

➢ We take credit for overcoming when a coach or teacher showed us how and we copied them.

As we take credit, we fail to see God's contributions through those people, and we are the poorer for it. This, my friend, is how God does it. This is how He grows us. He uses people, He uses things, and He uses circumstances. He uses events. He uses choices that we think are so bad to show us what is in us and where He is at work. It's All about Him.

Too often, we are the heroes of our own stories. We focus on us rather than God, and then we are surprised when we are powerless? But that is not our true heroes' reality. They focus on God as their power, and if we are our focus rather than Him, how can we be surprised?

When we are our heroes in our stories and our stories are imploding, then we are without hope in Someone greater Who works on our behalf to bring about His good work in us! How like Job we need an anchor, Someone to Whom we can appeal when life seems hard for us and for no one around us!

Look at one other place where God's sovereignty is so important!

Think about Peter's first missionary trip. Peter's first trip to take Christ to another culture would not have happened without God's softening up Peter. Remember the story? How did God soften up Peter? Let's look in the next chapter at how it transpired; remembering it's easier to see God's hand working when we look back instead of forward.

God Asks None of Us To Rescue His Reputation
When He is Transforming The World.

We saw God's Sovereignty when the world is exploding, when we know He is working in us, and when it feels personal. Now something amazing finds you. God is transforming the world and making "Transformers". Far beyond anything our children play with, God is making Transformers for His Kingdom.

When an army is about to move on the offensive, it first lets its artillery barrage the enemy lines where they will punch through. For hours or days the artillery and air force pound the enemy to break down defenses and open holes in the fortifications, then the offensive pours through that gap in the enemy's lines. It's called "softening up" the enemy line.

You are experiencing this as you read this book's pages. God is softening you up just as He did Peter.

Softening us up — Peter — I.A.A.H.[*]

God softened up Peter to send him to a new place beyond his culture, his thinking, and his comfort level. Here's how it happened.

The Holy Spirit moved in people's hearts in Caesarea. As God's Spirit drew Cornelius and others to God, He simultaneously

---

[*] It's All About Him. Come on, you guessed it right?

sent a dream to Peter to get him ready to go to these people. The timing was wonderful. Cornelius sent people who were on the road for a day to find the house where Peter was staying, and God repeated His dream to Peter three times (Peter was hard headed). The dream finished its third time just as Cornelius' messengers arrived!

The story shows us life in a Sovereign God's world. Notice:

- ɸ The Spirit changed lives in Caesarea apart from any apostle.[145]
- ɸ God moved Cornelius to send for a Christian (Peter).[146]

Problem: Peter's religion had trained him to know better than to mix with or eat with Cornelius' people.[147] Peter had to unlearn what religion had taught him so he could see God working.[148] God had to turn Peter's thinking around to use Him.

- ɸ The Holy Spirit sent a dream to cause Peter to unlearn his prejudices and open up to these people.[149]
- ɸ Cornelius' messengers arrived as Peter realized God prepared him for this trip.[150]
- ɸ Peter obeyed the Spirit's prompting to go with Cornelius' people.[151]
- ɸ Peter went with them, and if the triple dream had forced Peter to change his thinking, that could hardly compare to how God rocked Peter's boat next.
- ɸ Peter saw God working in people that Peter believed God cared nothing about! That stirred Peter unbelievably.
- ɸ Peter preached as God rocked his worldview. Now, look at what Peter said *about God*.[152]

God shows no favoritism. Vs. 34.

---

[145] Acts 10:1-2
[146] Acts 10:3-7
[147] Ezra 6:21 We talked about unlearning in Chapter 2.
[148] Acts 10:11-17
[149] Acts 10:17-20
[150] Acts 10:21
[151] Acts 10:23, 28-29
[152] Acts 10:34-43

- God chose people from every nation who fear Him. Vs. 35.
- God sent Israel His good news through Jesus Christ. Vs. 36.
- God anointed Jesus with the Holy Spirit and power. Vs. 38.
- God was with Jesus as He did good and healed people. Vs. 38.
- We witnessed everything Jesus did. Vs. 39.
- They killed Jesus (*the only thing men do in the sermon.*) Vs. 39.
- God raised Jesus from the dead. Vs. 40.
- People God had already chosen saw Jesus. Vs. 41.
- Jesus commanded us to preach. Vs. 42.
- God appointed Him as Judge of the living and the dead. Vs. 42.

Does that sound like it is about Peter or God? Do any of those things sound like Peter is preaching about himself rather than God?

- Peter saw what the Holy Spirit did among these strangers. [153]
- Peter saw the Holy Spirit come on them, just as on the Jews. [154]
- When he returned to hostile Jews in Jerusalem, Peter defended this new thing from God among gentiles simply: "So if God gave them the same gift as He gave us, who was I to think I could oppose God?" [155]

How many statements were about God in the above story? How many statements were about Peter? Can you see the profound difference between how Peter and the early church "transformers" talked and how we talk of God? We talk about us. We give God glancing nods. We ask Him to smile on our work, and we see God as a Heavenly slot machine. [156]

---

[153] Acts 10:2
[154] Acts 10:44-45
[155] Acts 10:47-48, 11:17
[156] I spoke at length about God not being our Heavenly slot machine in my chapter in *Conversations on Faith*, pages 181ff. (2004). Insight Publishing, Sevierville TN.

We take too much credit, and so we *see* God's work rarely. We praise people when we should praise God for what He is using their lives to do.

Preachers tell us, "You have to do this, and you have to do that." We hear how God works in a life because she was disciplined or he was self-sacrificing. It sounds like we are the straw that stirs the drink.

We take too much credit, and so we *see* God's work rarely. How much credit can we take for following Jesus? How much credit should we claim for surrendering our lives? We take the credit, so we think it is about us and we praise ourselves.

Ministers fit God's sovereignty into their belief systems. I heard one preach that God worked in Peter to prepare him for "the plan", and since Peter was submissive God used him. Did *Peter's* sermon sound like he focused on himself or his submission as much as today's preachers focus on Peter? Peter would point a finger and rage at such preachers, "How dare you move the focus onto me! You keep the focus on our great God or stop preaching!"

Jesus never apologized to Peter about making him a martyr, either. Peter's Master simply told him how he would die, and when Peter reached that terribly trying time, he responded that being crucified exactly as Christ had been crucified was too great an honor. Would they mind crucifying him upside down? And they did. For Peter, it was all about God, and Peter's affirmation that "Christ is Lord" is still today the foundation of Christ's Church.

Ultimate Transformation — Jesus in God's Sovereignty.

Up until Jesus' resurrection, people might be excused for thinking God's work in history was about Israeli real estate or being Jewish. Jesus cancelled all misconceptions by His words and actions on His last night before dying. He spoke of His death and *why* He was dying. He picked up a wine goblet and poured in wine saying, "this is My blood of the New Covenant, which ratifies the Agreement and is being poured out for many for the forgiveness of sins."[157] Jesus was surrendering (and would so many times on Good Friday!) to God's new covenant with us. Jesus didn't belabor His suffering. He wasn't self-serving about "His" part in God's plan. It was all about God, His Will, and His Plan — even for Jesus — especially for Jesus as He spoke of His dying.

Like Jesus, "all" we have to do is to stay, to remain, and to abide[158] in *God's agreement,* which is *the Covenant,* which is *God's Promise.* Whatever word we use — "testament", "accord", "calling" — God's Plan and His power to affect His Plan have always held center stage. God's Will was center stage all along.[159] His Plan was always here. We believe in Him who put the Plan into motion. True faith agrees with all He says He is. Prayer, faith, fulfillment, knowledge, and His love all reside in our agreement with a sovereign God. Joy, peace, power and grace are all in His Plan for us as His children: no begging, no pleading, and no worries. The Plan is His love, His promise. I.A.A.H.[160]

Fight This Truth — Please Don't Slipstream

What I am writing will find great opposition otherwise it wouldn't be as powerful as I know it is. It opposes much of what is taught everywhere. Do not just accept it. No one should simply believe it or instantly change his or her belief system, nor am I naive enough to believe most people will. Only those that are ready will see this truth, and they will be few. If you are one of

---

[157] Matthew 26:28
[158] John 15:1ff Jesus spoke on that last night of remaining in God, of abiding in Him.
[159] Matthew 12:20
[160] It's All About Him

them, please go to God's Word, and with an open heart, and praying only for truth, seek Him. Christ is the only Truth.[161] I don't know all truth, I only know Christ as Lord, and He is Truth.

I learned years ago that I couldn't teach anyone anything. I *can* challenge people to think, to study to show themselves approved by God.[162] And on the final day, "approved by God" will be everything!

We unconsciously develop our opposition as we form our belief systems, largely fostered by our parents or the church, or both. We then spend our lives hunting and seeing what supports our beliefs. In social research it is called confirmation bias, we look only for what confirms our bias. Can you imagine church leaders really opening up to what opposes their beliefs? For example, what would a minister do if he truly studied, sought truth, and embraced a different belief system? He would have to leave his church's safety, his denomination's circle, and his peers. Who will do so? Who will dare risk such challenges? I did that in 1969 and have never looked back. Why? Because God was leading me each step of the way, and I truly felt His presence.

I am confident that God will use this book to move in some lives, so that people can see Him. Is yours one of them? I know that is why He put His message in me to pass on to you. And as He moves you to see Him, to surrender to His Plan for your life it will be beautiful. Scary? Yes, but beautiful nonetheless.

Like us, most ministers slipstream in their beliefs. You see NASCAR racers slipstreaming often — following immediately behind the front car pushing against the wind. Many of us vote, believe, and socialize much the same as our parents or some earthly hero we latched onto — riding in their slipstream.

---

[161] John 14:6
[162] 2 Timothy 2:15

Jesus on His cross, out on Skull Hill was not slipstreaming. Jeremiah, Paul and Job never slipstreamed, nor did Luther or Calvin or the great missionaries. How do we slipstream?

Someone says something. We hear it and it creates a new image. The new image may be about us or someone else. As the person speaking creates that new image in us, it can form a self-image or if about someone else it forms a confirmation bias to help confirm the new image. That is why both gossip and well-deserved praise are so powerful! For example: someone mentions that a coworker "is always late." They may remark that without much evidence, but in time we hunt only the evidence that confirms our image of that coworker as always being late. We slipstreamed into the other person's image of that coworker.

Slipstreaming is dangerous in NASCAR. It is fatal for us.

This next take on a parable is unlike any you have heard. Check my work.[163]

Jesus' parable of the Good Samaritan reaches far beyond where it has been taken in the messages I have heard.

I think that preachers don't apply it like this because it necessitates taking a position where I believe our Christian community has been unwilling to go: *that we are victims to God.* Before I say this, remember the story of the man born blind. He was born that way according to Jesus "so that God's work might be displayed in his life." [164]

Now in the Good Samaritan's story, a beaten man was there for God to use for His glory. Look at the beaten man that the Samaritan found in Jesus' story.

> ➤ The beaten man in Christ's story was a victim as God planned for another's sin (the beating) to enter his life. Before you oppose this, think. Did the victim dictate his own creation? Did he ask to be born to be beaten? Would he have ever chosen

---

[163] 1 Thes. 5:21 — Test everything. Hold on to the good.
[164] John 9:3

that? No. Then how did it happen? God did it, pure and simple, for a reason, His reason.

- God put in all of them the needs that He knew would cause them to make each choice. None of them asked for any of the needs they had.

So Jesus said we are all victims to God, or *we are encountering victims,* and that is beautiful.

Again, we hear the parable preached because Jesus claimed that those in need have been put in their positions because man victimized them. But we have all been victimized and not just by people. We are *victims* for God's purposes just like the beaten man the Samaritan found. Like the beaten man —

- None of us chose for sin to exist.
- None of us chose our needs that cause us to fall to Satan's snares.
- We had nothing to do with God creating Satan.
- We didn't choose to be born into spiritual warfare.
- We didn't choose the fact that since the battle is spiritual that our only way to win is through God.

If we only fought flesh and blood, we might handle issues / battles ourselves. But it is spiritual warfare so we have no chance without God. He designed it that way. So, we choose God and His provisions or we are doomed. Thank you, God.

It is truly All About Him.

Returning to the story of the Good Samaritan, Jesus spoke of robbers, but how could robbers exist unless God allowed them? With God as our Protector, and He is — no robber harms us unless God allows it. None could. Period. Satan's effect on us is totally subject to God's allowing it to occur, just as in Job's life. Do you give Satan credit for what happens to you that you see as bad, which makes you just like Job's friends speaking into his life? Wrong. Satan is merely God's "water boy" to do His bidding. He does what God created him to do. God uses what he does to grow His children.

Do you take issue with this? I thought so. Then a good question is, "How is what you have been taught to believe working for you? For your family?" Are they slipstreaming into wrecks in their lives?

Are they struggling? Are their struggles and failures consistent with God's plan? Or does God's plan really offer joy, peace, and excitement in our walk even through life's struggles? This realization may feel as if a piano has been lifted from your shoulders.

Like Job, like the Prodigal, Paul told us that God never intended that we sin more and more![165] God forbid! We must see sin, as God sees it —"not counted to us."[166] We should hate sin, just as God does, but don't fear it. See sin as Satan's tool that God uses to grow His children.

> The price for all our 'rebellious freedom"
>
> was paid on a cross, and
>
> out of our thankfulness
>
> we respond to the love
>
> His grace puts in us
>
> to love Him.

As we embrace God's Plan and love, our desire diminishes for the sin that brings tears to His eyes. Yet in His process of growing us, our sovereign God understands sin's place in us. God truly wants us to center more on what He tells us, that we are His righteous ones. Why? Because of Him. Because of His price that makes us righteous.

So, how does God providentially see our sin?

God sees it as His tool to show us our need for Him, to show us our weakness without Him. Sin shows us our pride and moves us toward humility, which makes us more like Jesus. And God

---

[165] Romans 6:1
[166] Psalm 130:3; Jeremiah 31:34

also uses Satan's temptations at times, to show us growth that we didn't even know that God had done in us. When was the last time an old temptation reared its ugly head only for you to laugh and realize it no longer appealed to you? It's All About Him.

So look at the facts about sin.

FACTS:	
We do sin.	God does not.
We have sinned.	God cannot.
We will sin.	That is not part of the Father's Nature.

Who designed it that way? Did we? Did we choose sin before creation? Obviously no. God did. Then do we see sin as God does? Until we see sin as God does, we will struggle and experience more of the tool in our lives for God to grow us.

Question: Do we see ourselves as God does when we sin? Again, He sees us as righteous. Do we? He sees us as pure. Do we? He sees us wrapped in Jesus' righteousness.[167] And when we see us as He does, then we see — It's All About Him — and not our goodness, our dedication, or our discipline. If it was about us, we would get the glory — but all glory goes to God.

God sees our sin as rebellion. He does. But is that good or bad? When we confess (agree) that we're a sinner then we team with God to overcome it. So sin is bad (of course), but converted to good as God constructs us.

The question isn't, "Are we going to sin?" We know that one. The answer is not new as the Bible says: "We've compiled a long and sorry record as sinners and proved that we are utterly

---

[167] Romans 3:21-22, Romans 5:19, and Philippians 1:11

incapable of living the glorious lives God wills for us." [168] The question is, "Since we know that we sin, how does God see it?" He shows us the sin in our lives —

1) to show us *that we know* our need for His forgiveness, and / or
2) it is forgiven.

Those are all the possibilities as He grows us. There are no others.

Without sin, how would we grow? Why would we even need to grow? Wouldn't we be perfect? Why would we need a Savior? How could we even know we need one?

God is our Protector, and as such allows anything that happens in us to grow us, never, to harm us. Sin brings us to His bankruptcy court. Sin brings us to our knees; thoroughly convinced — It's All About Him.

God is sovereign.

He is not apologizing when the world explodes, when He works in someone, when it feels personal, or when He is transforming the world.

He patiently, lovingly awaits your responses to Him, knowing all along what each response will be. And you will favorably respond to Him, more and more, as He continues His work in you. Just as He promised. Just like His Word says.

---

[168] Romans 3:23 (MSG)

10

GOD-TOOLS FOR YOU
HE WASTES NOTHING

Jesus asked, "Do you believe that I am able to do this?"
"Yes, Lord," they replied. [169]
and He did it.

We tell stories only to forget how powerfully the stories illustrate God's truths. God never fails to equip us for what He calls us to do. He has tools. We are subject to His tools: so say our stories.

The problem is that we don't think in terms of equipment as we tell or live out our stories. We think of things we have or wish we had. We think of events as easy or hard things to endure.

We feel some things were wonderful and
some almost broke our hearts,
but liked or not,
all God's gifts come to equip us
because our Father loves us,
and God wastes nothing.
He wastes nothing.

He shapes and equips us for life. Think of it another way. I am touched and humbled by what our World War 2 veterans did against amazing odds. The stories of these brave men and women didn't center on whether they liked or disliked where they found themselves. We know that they would never have chosen

---

[169] Matthew 9:28-9

foxholes where their feet were soaked and rotting, and their hands were frostbitten as shells splintered forests around them, where they had no place to relieve themselves and no hot food for days. No, it was not about enjoyment but about what they did. God's astonishing tools are already in our lives. The question is, "How will we see His tools? Do we want them to work in us? Will we use them to His glory?" God — as all knowing and sovereign — has already answered these questions in each of our lives. We are on the learning curve, not God.

Read and enjoy, or think deeply, or grieve and let go, or pray and ask Him what to think. Again, pray. This chapter will not be easy for some people.

Not How The King Would Have Equipped Him

Tension floats on the wind with the battle flags of two armies lined up on opposite sides of the rocky, scraggly valley. Men have come out daily to face the prospect of death, lined up for battle and awaited the general's command to charge. They stood holding spears, shields, swords, rakes, pikes — or rocks.

Desperate, the king put his armor on a boy. This boy was the army's hope, which seems shameful, really. The boy said something, people heard him, they told others and before they knew it, the boy was trying to stand up, wearing the king's heavy armor. The king was tall. The boy was short, and in the king's armor he looked ridiculous. It was the boy who said, "This isn't going to work." He meant the armor. He left the armor.

The boy left the men and climbed down into the valley where a giant stood for the fortieth day, taunting the believers, laughing at their God, ridiculing their faith.

The boy had a slingshot, the kind that shepherds carry, and he stopped at a brook in the bottom of the canyon.

The giant noticed him and exploded in anger. Was this a crude joke? The "people of God" knew they could not beat him, so they sent a boy, a child! They sent the boy against him, a veteran, a proven warrior, a giant? This boy's death would somehow lessen him! Goliath roared out his anger.

The boy picked up five stones, smooth stones, aerodynamic, true in flight, not prone to lose velocity once they left his sling. He was told the giant had four brothers. Killing all five would make for a long day. This could be a long day.

Here is where you must answer the question. Do you believe that God gives us any job for which He has not, in His plan for our lives, equipped us?

Ask it another way: Do you believe God asks anything of us that He has not already given us the tools to accomplish?

Our answer as Christians lies in this and other stories.

The boy's name was David. He killed the giant with a single stone straight and true, buried in Goliath's skull between the eyes. The only one to hear the sound of the stone hitting his brain like a stone dropped in a pond was probably Goliath. That was the last thing he heard in this world, but it was not the last thing Goliath heard anyone say.

Do you know the last thing David said to Goliath? "You come at me with sword and spear and battle-ax. I come at you in the name of GOD-of-the-Angel-Armies, the God of Israel's troops, whom you curse and mock. This very day GOD is handing you over to me. I'm about to kill you, cut off your head, and serve up your body and the bodies of your Philistine buddies to the crows and coyotes. The whole earth will know that there's an extraordinary God in Israel. And everyone gathered here will learn that GOD doesn't save by means of sword or spear. The battle belongs to GOD — He's handing you to us on a platter!"[170]

Can you accept that God directed David's steps here, even here? Do you have a picture of God that is "so loving or so compassionate" that David could not boldly count that God

---

[170] 1 Samuel 17:45ff

directed his steps here, here of all places where David most needed Him?

God equipped David, but not as King Saul or Goliath would have equipped a champion. No, not as the experienced warriors would have equipped a boy, but as God desired, as a Sovereign God chose to equip him and use him. Did God ever use him!

God used David's young years.

He used David's encounters with bears and lions,

God used David's lonely hours with a scrawny herd of sheep, and his gumption.

God used David's tendency to spout off, to ask too many questions, to get noticed and — improbably — to kill a giant.

God also used David's humility. David knew that only God could pull off this upset.

Listen to him again,

"GOD is handing you over to me."

"GOD doesn't save by means of sword or spear."

"The battle belongs to GOD."

I am saying that God equipped David properly. That amazing day David had all the tools he needed for God's purposes. God equipped David with each and every one of those "tools".

Many Christian teachers agree on most of God's tools that He uses to shape us as vessels of mercy to His glory. They preach these in sermons and I agree with everyone about the good tools: spiritual gifts,[171] personality, talents, Spiritual Armor,[172] forgiveness, and the Fruit of the Spirit.[173]

Where I differ is that I believe God designed the other list that teachers teach as the *opposite* of the Spirit's work. We speak as if we created the other list — those sins of our sinful nature that

---

[171] Romans 12, Ephesians 4, and 1 Corinthians 12
[172] Ephesians 6:10-19
[173] Galatians 5:23-24

Satan plays to — and that lie somehow makes us a little more proud of them. Look at the other tools God uses in us:[174]

The acts of the sinful nature are obvious:
sexual immorality,
impurity and
debauchery
idolatry and
witchcraft;
hatred,
discord,
jealousy,
fits of rage,
selfish ambition,
dissensions,
factions
envy;
drunkenness,
orgies, and the like.

Paul finished the powerful, frightening list with — I warn (really the word is *warn*) you, as I did before, that those who live like this will not inherit the kingdom of God."

What Paul wrote quiets us.

Sin is a killer. It is deadly serious. It can cost you your life, relationships, health, and any joy in this world. It is no laughing matter. At no time in this book have I, nor will I, ever make light of it. Nor will I lessen my responsibility for my sin before my Father. Never.

My point is simple. God knew sin would come into the Garden of Eden because He designed sin — to teach us. In a believer, in a child of God, in someone who has clung to Christ as Lord of his or her life, sin has a purpose. I won't talk of sin for the rest of the world, but God uses anything He chooses to draw people to Himself or to make us more like Him.

Let's look at the sin list again, shall we? But this time, we are simply going to compare the list that follows a few verses later

---

[174] Galatians 5:18ff

in Galatians 5:22-23. We quote them here so you can see the comparison. God directed Paul to write:

"But the fruit of the Spirit is love, joy, peace, patience, kindness, goodness, faithfulness, gentleness and self-control. Against such things there is no law." I add verse 24 so you can see the process. "Those who belong to Christ Jesus have crucified the sinful nature with its passions and desires."

The sin or more precisely "act of the sinful nature"	The corresponding Fruit of the Spirit
sexual immorality ▶	Love, patience
Impurity ▶	Love, goodness
Debauchery ▶	Love, kindness
Idolatry ▶	Faithfulness, goodness
Witchcraft ▶	Joy, faithfulness
Hatred ▶	Love, peace, gentleness
Discord ▶	Goodness, self-control
Jealousy ▶	Love, joy, self-control
fits of rage ▶	Self-control, patience
selfish ambition ▶	Kindness, joy
Dissensions ▶	Self-control, patience
Factions ▶	Love, patience
Envy ▶	Goodness, Faithfulness
Drunkenness ▶	Goodness, Self-Control
Orgies ▶	Love, Self-Control
and the like ▶	All of them, I guess!

Every sin is *on the way to*, or *in the way of* something good, something Christlike that God wants to birth in us. Paul tried to tell us that clinging to the wrong thing, sin, kept us from letting go of it and letting God bring out His Spirit's true Fruit in us.

Look at verse 24 again, please. Don't miss this: "Those who belong to Christ Jesus have crucified the sinful nature with its passions and desires." When sin has shown us our horror, our sickness, our desire to be gods, then we confess it. We agree with God that it is killing us, stealing our fellowship with Him, and hate it. Then God does what we could not:

He forgives us.

He cleanses us from all unrighteousness and THEN

He builds in us what we were looking for with all of our sinning: "love, joy, peace, patience, kindness, goodness, faithfulness, gentleness and self-control."

That is beautiful beyond words, and that process will play over and over in our lives until the day of our redemption.

So What Am I Saying About "Tools"?

God uses two toolkits: one set for deconstructing and another set for constructing a saint, for making a son or daughter to more than look like Jesus. God wants us to become more and more like Jesus.

We find some tools in both toolkits. We may find one tool in the deconstructing toolkit, but we also see it in the construction toolkit, which makes sense. People who tear down houses use hammers, but so do people who frame the new house to replace the old one.

What are some of the tools we find in both toolkits? We find temptation/testing, relationships, tragedies, and calling in both of God's toolkits: deconstructing and constructing.

Tools we find in both toolkits —

We find the Temptation / testing tool in deconstructing *and* constructing took kits. Temptation / testing brings out both our sin and whatever victories we enjoy in God. Please know that the Greek word for tempt and test is the same word — *peirazo* — or *scrutinize, entice, assay, examine, prove, tempt* or *try*. When God allows us to be tempted or He tests us,

He assays what is truest of us,

He proves to us what our inner reality is.

He scrutinizes, and allows us to see what is in us.

If Christians fail a temptation or test, then we see a place for His Holy Spirit to change us. When we find that an assay shows a good quality, we are amazed — God's grace has changed us, has saved another piece of us for His glory.

Another tool we find in both toolkits is relationships. The Bible tells us that a positive influence is beyond beautiful. "A friend loves at all times, and a brother is born for adversity."[175] How wonderful when a friend loves us even when we hate ourselves! How amazing when we feel defeated and broken to have a brother lift us up, stand in the cesspool with us, or refuse to leave us drowning in our sin!

Those relationships are wonderful, but the opposite is equally true. Some people show our worst side. With some we lose self-control, we rage, we get filthy mouthed, or party to excess. The Bible warns that some people reduce us: "the prostitute reduces you to a loaf of bread."[176] Some people reduce us to objects for them to use and throw away. They make us cheap. Those relationships are powerful tools to deconstruct us.

So relationships appear in both the tearing-down and building-up toolkits. What else do we find in both kits? In both toolkits we find tragedy, sickness, and every evil that has touched us. The world is filled with people who are wrecked, angry about it, and festering. They are angry with God, so it is hard to determine whether they are being built up, or broken down, or going nowhere. God knows. We trust His plan for them. So we find terrible things, feared things in the deconstructing toolkit.

But we also find tragedy in God's building kit, beautifully timed in lives to transform souls to look like His Son. So many saints — Oswald Chambers, Athanasius, Martin Luther, John

---

[175] Proverbs 17:17
[176] Proverbs 6:26

Calvin, Teresa of Avila and Joan of Arc — all told us that tragedy and pain were God's tools to build them up in God's grace. Paul[177], Peter[178], and James[179] told us to endure[180] hardships. Moreover they said to rejoice when life's bottom fell out from heartbreaks, disillusionments, and tribulation, because these things kept them in unmoved devotion to God. These things prove that God is truest when life is most difficult. God is strongest when life is craziest. God's love shines through most brilliantly in life's darkest recesses.

Again, we find tragedies and sadness in both toolkits, and I would like to point to another tool we can find in both kits: calling. We find our sense of calling, our trust that God is working in us to make us what He purposed us to be in both toolkits.

Maybe God called you to be a doctor, and that is good, but doctors can abort babies, or sell needless prescriptions or addictive medicines to patients. Doctors can perform needless surgeries, be so arrogant that they think they are God, and damage people irreparably. The calling of "doctor" can be destructive. Similarly doctors diagnose so brilliantly that they give back lives, prolong marriages, and restore helpless souls. Amazingly, some doctors counsel patients to find Christ and find health in the Great Physician for the first time.

Do you see how calling can be destructive or constructive? God may use your sense of calling to finish tearing down lies in you. He may use your calling to build your character and pass blessings through you.

I am a lawyer and know other lawyers, both men and women, who make me proud to wear that calling. They truly seek to serve clients, to better lives, to redress wrongs, and courageously to fight criminality. Just as easily, I know those who bully people, gouge

---

[177] Romans 5:3-5
[178] 2 Peter 1:5-8
[179] James 1:2-5
[180] 2 Timothy 2:10

the innocent, and serve only their own pocket books. God has every one of them where they must be, either to prove His salvation in them, or show them their desperate need of a Savior, or show a Christian where his Lord desires to work next in his life.

This principle of destroy and build for calling seems truer for the call to preach. Clearly, God warned teachers[181] and church leaders[182] or servants[183] to be held to higher standards. That doesn't mean that we build them pedestals, but we have all seen that some treasure their call from God. They bring it honor. My dad was one of those people.

He was a hard worker: holding down at least two and sometimes three jobs. Often in cotton growing season, dad's only sleep came in a field for as many as five nights in a row, tending our crop after he came home from selling cars. He caught naps on an irrigation ditch's bank late in the night. My father never believed that his walk with God focused on what God would do for Him. He lived his strong faith and trusted God to do what He would do. Dad drove us long distances to fill pulpits for churches without pastors. He never complained. We lost our cotton crop one year, which was the largest part of our income. I never heard him plead with God to do something or make things easy. I assume that my father never called a prayer chain to help him beg God for what he wanted. That was my dad, my hero whose life revealed Christ in a big way.

At the same time some preach the words, quote the Bible, and say that God speaks to them, but they do not unite with those who suffer. They make money and draw attention to themselves. They give God's call to preach a bad name. I saw in a recent survey that among 75 jobs people respected or trusted, preachers only ranked above some criminal activities! It is beautiful if the Lord breaks a false preacher, shows him his error or resurrects her to preach His

---

[181] James 3:1
[182] 1 Timothy 3:1ff
[183] 1 Timothy 3:8ff

Truth fully and not commercially. If they do not come to such a place, if they aren't part of those God elected, they will find themselves before Jesus trying to impress Him with their works in His name, only to hear Him say, "I never knew you."[184]

Do you see how God uses "calling" to dissolve us, bulldoze our lies, or deconstruct our favorite ways of deceiving ourselves? Do you see equally how He can use our calling to build Jesus into us?

Another way to say this is that these tools are neither good nor bad. They are neutral. God uses even our negative reactions to these tools. God can use them as He chooses, but our positive reaction to these tools opens us up to God; open us up to His Plan in our lives. Either way, It's All About Him.

Some tools, though, destroy garbage in our lives. How grateful we must be for these destructive agents in God's arsenal of Grace to us. Let's look at them.

Get Out The Wrecking Ball, God's Working Again

I am going to talk about the deconstructing tools now. They alert us that God is working in new parts of our lives. When you first came to Christ, you came with sin that had brought you down, scared you, or emptied your joy.

Have you watched the Discovery Channels shows where contractors demolish buildings? I marvel as they stripped an old hotel of everything recyclable. Then they doze and clear away interior walls to orchestrate how the building collapses in on itself. Next they drill to place explosives and wire, then connect them to precise timing devices. All the while they shield nearby buildings and work to protect surrounding areas. Finally, on a weekend day, police control crowds and the contractors set off the timers. If you

---

[184] Matthew 7:21-23

have seen the interior shots (how do they film that?) you can see inside columns blasted in two, floors buckle, the interior begin to fall, and then all the walls collapse in on themselves. The hotel falls down and at the same time falls away from the surrounding buildings into and onto itself.

Dust billowed for blocks forming a plume in the sky, but a space was instantly vacated. Rubble crews hauled away the remains. Soon, new crews excavated a new foundation, and then steel people came welding to form a backbone and limbs for the new structure.

Like those demolition crews, God deconstructs us in huge, overwhelming moments. Again, like the building implosion crews, He has worked for days, months, or even decades to remove all the lies and crumbling sin to reveal how hollow we were, how profoundly we need Him to build something new in us.

The first destructive tool is, as I have said, sin. Now, imagine Christians who believe that even their sin is in God's hand to finish the good work He began in them, and promised to complete in them. It was a hard step for me.

As I worked on this book's core concept, I finally saw it clearly enough to tell my guys at the Cigar Shop. They asked about its title. I said I would tell them, but added that I wasn't in a mood to defend it. I just wanted them to think about it.

I told them: "Satan — God's designed tool to grow His children."

I was blown away. They are knowledgeable and strongly opinionated. They crazily agreed, "It makes sense!"

"That's it! It explains so much."

"Unbelievable."

Their reaction amazed me. These guys follow no one. I carefully continued to pursue and pray through these thoughts.

I called my youngest son to tell him. He got it right away, was blown away, and called me back twice with questions and input. I aired the ideas with others, to let their questions sharpen my thoughts, and force me to ground them in scripture.

As I said earlier, seminary-trained preachers had the most difficulty, because they realized that teaching radical truth might cost them their livelihood. But many others were strengthened to walk for our Loving Father.

So what other tools does God desire to use in us to destroy old works, old lies, old parts of our nature that do not resemble Christ? I want you to look at "the eradicators" that God has so graciously provided because He loves us. These demolish old attachments to past sin.

The Eradicators

The tools that most people fail to see or use are what I call the Eradicators. When I hand my sin back to God, every aspect of it, then I find something totally unexpected. God, in His Plan for my life also brought —

A Guilt Eradicator,

A Fear Eradicator, and

A Care/Anxiety Eradicator

Let's look at them.

THE GUILT ERADICATOR First, Guilt is antithetical to God's purposes, to His desire to build His image in us. I see that much of religion runs on guilt. Too many preachers play to guilt, but look at how God taught us to see guilt.

First, guilt is so intermixed with sin that the same biblical words are often translated either way. In fact, if you read the King James Version of the Bible you won't see "guilt" but twice in the whole Bible! Only in our more recent versions do we see a greater precision in the two words. In the Law of Moses, we see that anyone who sinned brought two sacrifices. He "confessed in what way he had sinned"[185] and as a penalty for the sin, he brought two animals[186] for a sin offering. The two sacrifices atoned for (paid for) his sin, so he was forgiven[187] of the sin *and* the guilt. But he might unintentionally sin.[188] He then brought a guilt offering to "make restitution for what he failed to do in regard to the holy things."[189]

See something powerful. Sin was something they did knowingly. Guilt came from "ignorant, unknowing things" that someone pointed out to a believer later. Have you ever said, "If only I had known, I would never have..." and the weight of that unwitting hurt to someone else was so heavy? That is guilt.

Guilt is 1) sin's leftover weight in us. Guilt is also 2) a weight we carry for unknowingly sinning. Paul paints it this way. Sin is the infraction, and guilt is the ongoing debt.[190] Either way you can see how we build houses of guilt and live in our guilt like a house full of radon, allergens, mold and harmful chemicals.

Enter God's Guilt Eradicator. See it in someone you know.

King David was drowning under twin weights of adultery and murder; "My guilt has overwhelmed me like a burden too heavy to bear."[191] Guilt broke him. Guilt did God's desired work in David and brought him to the end of himself where he finally "acknowledged my sin to You and did not cover up my iniquity. I said, 'I will confess my transgressions to the Lord' — and *You forgave the guilt of my sin*." David no longer had to carry the weight of guilt. He no longer had to wear the taint of guilt.

God eradicated David's guilt. God cleansed him and freed him from it. Now Satan will bring back our guilt, but Satan gambles in doing so. He hopes that you won't take your guilt to

---

[185] Leviticus 5:5
[186] Leviticus 5:6
[187] Leviticus 5:10
[188] Leviticus 5:15
[189] Leviticus 5:16
[190] Romans 3:24ff, Ephesians 1:7, Colossians 1:14
[191] Psalm 38:4

the Light; you will try to cover it and in so doing keep it festering in your inner darkness: stifling you, sucking your life from you.

Confess the sin and lose the guilt. Let God eradicate them from you. Jesus died to eradicate your useless weight of guilt.

For some of us, guilt goes deeper; we feel we inherited it from our family. We see it in the Bible[192] people confessed the sin of their parents and generations before them. The weight, the legacy of that generational sin kept them down.

So what do we know? The Holy Spirit came to "convict the world of guilt in regard to sin and righteousness and judgment."[193] God shines His light on our guilt and tells us that this weight is in the way of His building something new into us — righteousness and good judgment. He wants to eradicate the guilt.

God then invites us: "draw near with a sincere heart in full assurance of faith, having our hearts sprinkled to cleanse us from a guilty conscience!"[194]

God uses guilt to show us our sin or something we missed.

God then eradicates the guilt once it does its job. Do unhealthy forms of guilt abound in us? Yes, ask a doctor how ill guilt can make us.

Is guilt beautiful when it does its job and brings us to God to destroy some old sin in us? Yes!

Then God eradicates the guilt. Just like a crew demolishing an old hotel to build a new one. God does not want us to build a new hotel and fill its rooms with debris that used to occupy the site!

God has His Guilt Eradicator ready to go, but that's not all. God has a Fear Eradicator.

THE FEAR ERADICATOR In my first book, *The Verdict Is In: Fear is Never Your Friend*[195] I spoke about this at length. God

---

[192] Jeremiah 14:20
[193] John 16:8
[194] Hebrews 10:22

never intended us to live in fear or guilt. Let me point to what God's Word says about fear, and if you need more help with this, please read my first book. Not only will you learn once and for all that fear is not your friend, you will also learn how you replace fear with two positives: knowledge and wisdom. I wish space permitted me to share some of the letters and emails I have received from people saying their lives have changed since reading my book on fear.

Just look at these promises about God's Fear Eradicator. IF WE HAVE CHRIST AS LORD —

We won't fear, though the earth gives way and the mountains fall into the heart of the sea.[196]

Why should we fear when evil days come?[197]

We won't fear the terror of night, nor the arrow that flies by day.[198]

Our hearts are secure. We will have no fear.[199]

We won't fear sudden disaster or the ruin that overtakes the wicked.[200]

Not only should we expect God to eradicate the fear in our lives, but also we join His Fear Eradication team. He invites us to "say to those with fearful hearts, 'Be strong, do not fear. Your God will come… to save you.'"[201]

When we forget, He reminds us, "So do not fear, for I am with you. Do not be dismayed, for I am your God. I will strengthen you and help you; I will uphold you with My righteous right hand."[202]

---

[195] Richardson, G.L. (2006). *The Verdict is In: Fear Is Never Your Friend.* (Honor Net Publishing, Sapulpa, OK) To order go to —
[196] Psalm 46:2
[197] Psalm 49:5
[198] Psalm 91:5
[199] Psalm 112:8
[200] Proverbs 3:25
[201] Isaiah 35:4
[202] Isaiah 41:10

Not enough? Then hear it from the apostles. Paul says, "God did not give us a spirit of timidity, but a spirit of power, of love and of self-discipline."[203] John adds: "There is no fear in love. But [His] perfect love drives out fear, because fear has to do with punishment. The one who fears is not made perfect in love."[204]

God is making us like Jesus: perfect. We won't be perfect in this world, but He is not abandoning His project. He is still making us "perfect in His love" and that means Fear Has Been Eradicated.

Fear was cleared off the building site along with guilt. God doesn't need them. He won't use them in building His daughters or His sons.

God has a Guilt and a Fear Eradicator in His Toolkit, but that is not all. He also carries and uses a Care / Anxiety Eradicator. Please allow me to tear apart two things that are closely related, but which are not the same. That word for 'care' is *not* like the word for loving care — *agape*.

THE CARE/ANXIETY ERADICATOR No, this word for care / anxiety means *to disunite, to differ, to distract*. So hear God clearly, "Cast all your anxiety, all your distractions, everything that splits you down the middle on Him because He cares for you."[205]

You say, "I know that I am distracted, that I am anxious, but honestly, I am not even sure what my anxieties are!" David experienced this. He asked God to send His Care/Anxiety Eradicator when he could not even know his own heart: "Search me, O God, and know my heart; [You] test me and know my anxious thoughts." David asked God to ferret them out, to find his cares and banish his anxious thoughts because they were hidden from him! How amazing is that?

---

[203] 2 Tim. 1:7
[204] 1 John 4:18
[205] 1 Peter 5:7

You ask, "How do I help to bring the eradicators to my loved ones?" This is simple, "An anxious heart weighs a man down, but a kind word cheers him up."[206]

You ask, "Can we truly ask God to eradicate care / anxiety from us?" Again, God says, "So, banish anxiety from your heart and cast off the troubles of your body, for youth and vigor are meaningless."[207] When our anxiety-ridden world lies to us and tells us to get face lifts, tucks, and anything to 'preserve youth' rather than going to the heart of the aging that heals our souls, we should stand and say, "We as children of our Loving Father have a care / anxiety eradicator! It is His love. It is resting in His plan for us."

You say, "Okay, I need something stronger than telling me to 'banish' my anxieties." I agree. So here, "Don't be anxious about anything, but in everything, by prayer and petition, with thanksgiving, present your requests to God."[208] To begin my prayers and petitions; I wrap them; I anchor them in thanksgiving. Thanksgiving is how I remember all those ways that He has been faithful to me in the past. He gave me back my eyesight, gave me rest when sleep was denied, brought me through two divorces and caused me to flourish, to find His joy, to learn, to be alive! How many people passing through divorces desperately need to *know* that God is directing their steps *especially* in those dark nights! When I get started on all of those things for which I am thankful, both the good and the seemingly bad at the time:

How can I be anxious? Look Who has led me all the way and will lead me Home!

How can I be fearful? Look Who holds my hand!

How can I be guilt ridden? Look Who paid my "tab" with Satan!

---

[206] Proverbs 12:25
[207] Eccles. 11:10
[208] Philip. 4:6

It is right here that so many preachers ring false. They sell Christianity as if they were selling a car they had never driven, much less owned. It is as if they sell a used car and their haircut and cheap suit are telling you, "Buyer beware! He's lying!" I am not out to write a theological treatise. I can only tell you that I sleep at night. I enjoy my days. I have joy, such joy because He has redeemed even my worst sin. He is continually eradicating my fears, guilt, and care/anxiety from my life! All of my life, all of my actions, all of my nights have been in His plan, in His foreknowledge, and like David, such knowledge is too wonderful for me![209] Even when David (and you and I) are despicable and failing — God directs. No conditions. God directs. God never quits directing. Such unconditional love is too amazing.

So God uses tools that fit in both the deconstruction and the construction toolkits. Some tools fit in the destruction toolkit — the eradicators. Some have been written about for eons as God's construction tools to build new things in us.

Eradicators: Think of them another way.

Think of eradicators one other way. Let's look at fear by itself, and at guilt with care / anxiety.

Look at fear first. You say, "Scripture tells us to 'fear God,'" and you are right. It says that, but their words in Hebrew and Greek are more precise than ours, and mean very different things. Look at what the Bible says with me.

God told Abraham after he showed his faithfulness even to sacrificing Isaac, "Now I know that you fear God." [210]

Joseph told his brothers why they could trust that he would not take revenge on them — "for I fear God."[211]

---

[209] Psalm 139:6
[210] Genesis 22:12
[211] Genesis 42:18

Moses knew Pharaoh was lying about releasing the Israelites and was in trouble because he "still did not fear the Lord God."[212]

That word for fear was the Hebrew's word *yaré*, which meant awe and reverence. Want to see their different words for fear? Let's look at verses that put *fear* versus *God's reverence* into perspective.

First, look at what Moses says when the Israelites come to Mount Sinai, which is wrapped in God's presence. Moses tells them, "Do not be afraid. God has come to test you, so that *the fear of God* will be with you to keep you from sinning."[213] God was telling them, "Don't be afraid like children or animals, but reverence God like wise adults."   Second, look at what happened when a godly king, Jehoshaphat went into battle praising God. God delivered him miraculously from three nations assembled against him! What happened? "The fear of God came upon all the [surrounding] kingdoms when they heard how the Lord had fought against the enemies of Israel."[214] Those surrounding kingdoms that did not worship or love God were induced to *dread* God and hold God in terror.

See two forms of fear.

For those of us who love Him — reverence and awe.

For everyone else — dread.

God underscores this difference between fear and awe another way, God said through a prophet, Isaiah, "So do not fear, for I am with you; do not be dismayed, for I am your God."[215]

---

[212] Exodus 9:30
[213] Exodus 20:20
[214] 2 Chron. 20:29
[215] Isaiah 41:10

Further God said, "I am the Lord, your God, Who takes hold of your right hand and says to you, do not fear."[216]

A satanic priest explained it this way. Satan knows he can't have our worship as saints, so he feeds on, he thrives on "worship's back door" — fear, dread, and terror as some of his choice methods. Satan loves horror movies; they give him a buzz. Satan takes the counterfeit of good things: happiness for joy, sexual satiation for oneness with our intended. He does the same for worship — settling for dread.

What about guilt, care / anxiety? I already shared some verses with you, but think of having sin pointed out to you in this way. When I sin, only four beings can point out my sin to me. Two of the possibilities are human: others and me. The other two to point out a sin are God and Satan. If it is God, then I know why His Holy Spirit points out sin. It's spelled out in His job description from Jesus. Read this and let it wash through you. "When [the Holy Spirit] comes, He'll expose the error of the godless world's view of sin, righteousness, and judgment: He'll show them that their refusal to believe in Me is their basic sin."[217] The Spirit only points out sin *to get us to Truth.* He points out sin *to ferret it out.* The Holy Spirit only brings Light to sin to abolish it, to let us live.

The Holy Spirit points it out to get rid of it.

Before I talk about Satan and his role as accuser, let me say that in my 32 years as a trial attorney, I have served on both sides of the aisle. I served as an Assistant District Attorney and as the United States Federal Prosecutor for the Eastern District of Oklahoma, appointed by then President Ronald Reagan to prosecute Federal criminal cases against the accused.

In doing so I have learned two things in trial proceedings that help me understand Satan's role, as opposed to the Holy Spirit's

---

[216] Isaiah 41:13
[217] John 16:8-9

role. The two things are discovery and what I call "the story" of a case.

Discovery In discovery, each side brings its evidence to be admitted into the trial itself and submits it to the court and jury. Each side wants to bring the evidence that corroborates its version of the facts, of the evidence to be admitted to the trial itself. Hear this: Jesus' blood covers our sin. That doesn't mean it didn't happen, but it means that our sin is no longer admissible in God's court of opinion and judgment of us as His children.[218] In God's court, when Satan dredges up old garbage for which we have asked for and received God's forgiveness, all of it is disqualified in the discovery process for the trial of our lives as His children in God's judgment! So the process of discovery as evidence is admitted and disqualified is important to understanding the role of Jesus in our lives. He covers and disqualifies our sin from God's consideration. Wow. How beautiful is that?

This has been so practical to me as a trial lawyer. Unlike most lawyers, I *never* worry myself with the opponent's case, only to know what it is. I focus on my case. Lawyers never believe me on this unless they try a case with me and there they see it first hand. I focus solely on the facts of my case and work off the Truth that I see Jesus as our Advocate using — that when I sell my facts to the jury, it won't matter what the other side does. I do not think Christ bothers with what Satan wants to drag up. It has no value, no importance, because His blood has deleted it. I never see myself in a courtroom as a defender. I am on the offense, presenting my case. My record speaks for itself. Go to richardsonlawfirmpc.com and see for yourself.

The Story But that is not all. When I sit in a trial, my job is to hear all that is being said, while not letting what is being said cause me to change my focus and plan. If I operate with truth, I stay with truth and truth is always, in the end, what succeeds. I

---

[218] Jeremiah 31:34

know, you think, "Not always!" Yes, in the end, always!! In the same way that God doesn't counter or react to Satan — God moves on with His truth — so do I. I often have a story, my working interpretation of the facts as we begin, but I must clearly understand *the* story, Truth, that takes into account both my client's and the opponent's sides of the story.

God does that in a marvelous, shockingly beautiful manner.

He deletes our sin, covered and forgiven as part of His plan, He bases our case on what Jesus did on the cross for us

He deletes what Satan *cannot* accuse us of doing because it is inadmissible, it is forgiven, Jesus covered it.

But God takes into account HIS STORY of our lives.

God weighs most heavily His Story, His account, His view of the facts of our lives. God knows His Story because it's His Plan for our lives! Satan's "story" is irrelevant when God forgives us.

He will render a verdict for us.

Now look at what Satan tries and what he cannot accomplish, *unless we are ignorant.*

Why does Satan bring up forgiven sin in us? He knows he can't bring up our sin to God, as God knows the truth, that the sin was forgiven the instant we confessed it. So does Satan want to get rid of any of our sin? No! Never! He wants our sin to fester. He wants our guilt to rot in us. He hopes our fear eats away at us. He wants our care/anxiety to bring death.

So when you look at a sin, and its guilt and anxiety are wearing you down — and you know that the Holy Spirit only points it out so you can let Him cut it out like a surgeon and bring healing. You know that the Holy Spirit brings it to your attention so you can bring it to Jesus who died for it and wants you to learn from it and live, to be forgiven and flourish. That is God's Plan! That is God's infinite love!

So are you still languishing in guilt, in fear, and in care/anxiety? Guess who wants that?

Deny that to the enemy. Cling to Christ. Let Him forgive and cleanse you from all unrighteousness![219]

Read God's Blueprint:
All of These Build His New Life in Us

God also has a plethora, a spread of tools to build us, to construct us, to fortify us for living victoriously in Him.

I am no expert on these. Other writers and Christian brothers and sisters have often spent their life's work studying some of these, and you should listen to them, read them, and study God's Word and what *He says* about these more than anyone else.

> *Ask and it will be given to you; seek and you will find; knock and the door will be opened to you. For everyone who asks receives; he who seeks finds; and to him who knocks, the door will be opened.* Jesus

God tells us to ask Him for things even though He already knows our needs and has already made provision for them. He still wants us to ask, as this is apparently part of our relationship and connection with Him. In fact, God took it as a sure sign that King Ahaz was an unbeliever, not His child when he refused to ask Him for anything.[220] So God says —

Ask for the ancient paths, ask where the good way is, and walk in it. [221]

Ask God to interpret your dreams. [222]

Ask the Lord of the harvest to send out workers into His harvest. [223]

If two of you agree about anything you ask for, it will be done for you by my Father in heaven. [224]

---

[219] 1 John 1:9
[220] Isaiah 7:11-12
[221] Jeremiah 6:16
[222] Daniel 2:23
[223] Matthew 9:38
[224] Matthew 18:19

"If you believe, you will receive whatever you ask for in prayer." [225]

And I will do whatever you ask in My name, so that the Son may bring glory to the Father. [226] (God works in us to even bring about our desire to "believe".)

We pray for you and ask God to fill you with the knowledge of His will. [227]

If you lack wisdom, ask God, Who gives generously to all without finding fault, and it will be given to you. [228]

Paul told us how God started directing him so that he knew it from the first. God had just struck Paul blind on the road to Damascus.

" 'What shall I do, Lord?' I asked.

" 'Get up,' the Lord said, 'and go into Damascus. There you will be told all that you have been assigned to do.'" [229]

Wow! Don't you wish God spoke to us like that every day? Maybe you have asked God for something, and you don't feel that you got what you asked from Him. I know. Me too.

So how do we improve our "askers"? How do we grow wiser, or more like Jesus in what we ask God? Here are some questions that Jesus asks in return to help you grasp what it means to be conformed to His image. Jesus asks us:

"Do you believe that I am able to do this?"[230]

"Have you understood all these things?" [231]

"Are you still so dull?" [232] Ouch.

"But what about you? Who do you say I am?" [233]

---

[225] Matthew 21:22
[226] John 14:13-14
[227] Col. 1:9
[228] James 1:5-6
[229] Acts 22:10
[230] Matthew 9:28
[231] Matthew 13:51
[232] Matthew 15:16
[233] Matthew 16:15

"What is it you want?" Jesus asked.

She answered Him.

Jesus replied, "You don't know what you are asking," [234]

"What do you want me to do for you?" [235]

"Why are you thinking these things in your hearts? [236]

"Where is your faith?"[237]

"Do you *want* to get well?" [238]

Where are your accusers? Has no one condemned you?" [239]

With these insights, God refined the asking element of our relationship. Let them speak to you. They strengthen me when I need it. They haunt me when I must be reminded I am rebelling in what I ask. They bring me back to the heart of my request when it fails to line up with His heart. Read each one, one at a time, and savor them. Let them percolate down into your spirit.

If you remain in Me and my words remain in you, ask whatever you wish, and it will be given you. [240]

In that day you will ask in My name. I am not saying that I will ask the Father on your behalf. [241]

"Do you love me?" [242] — Jesus.

I keep asking that God, the glorious Father, may give you the Spirit of wisdom and revelation, so that you may know Him better. [243]

Now to Him Who is able to do immeasurably more than all we ask or imagine, according to His power that is at work within us. [244]

---

[234] Matthew 20:20-22
[235] Matthew 20:32
[236] Luke 5:22
[237] Luke 8:25
[238] John 5:6
[239] John 8:10
[240] John 15:7
[241] John 16:26
[242] John 21:17
[243] Ephes. 1:17
[244] Ephes. 3:20

When you ask, you do not receive, because you ask with wrong motives, that you may spend what you get on your pleasures. [245]

We receive from Him anything we ask, because we obey His commands and do what pleases Him. [246]

This is our confidence in approaching God: If we ask anything according to His will, He hears us. And if we know that He hears us — whatever we ask — we know that we have what we asked of Him. [247]

Again, God tells us to ask Him for things. God's Word, His beautiful blueprint for our lives holds some things, which we never have to ask for. They are ours as His children. Already promised. Already at our disposal. Already poised to aid us in our lives to His glory. You probably know these.

ARMOR — God has given us ample protection.[248]

FRUIT — the core of our character is a gift, is a result of our fellowship with Him. [249]

GIFTS — All good gifts are from God for us as His children.[250]

GIVING — we have more than enough to give in His name. [251]

PRAYER — As much as we breathe and walk, we should be praying.

SPIRITUAL GIFTS — We each have a unique blend of Gifts for ministering in His name. [252]

WITNESSING — He loves each of us so much that we are His salt and light for this world. [253]

CHARACTER — as we walk with our Father, we become like Him. [254]

---

[245] James 4:3
[246] 1 John 3:22
[247] 1 John 5:14-15
[248] Ephesians 6:10-20
[249] Galatians 5:22-4
[250] Mathew 7:11; James 1:17
[251] 2 Corinthians 9:7
[252] Romans 12:6ff; I Corinthians 12-14; Ephesians 4:8ff
[253] Acts 1:6-8
[254] Romans 5:4

Many teachers and preachers teach us to petition God. But what I see God showing us in His word seems different from what we hear from too many pulpits. I believe God isn't impressed with how many of His children beg Him to do a certain thing in someone's life, rather than what He knows is best. We can trust Him for what is best. In doing so, God gets the glory, not a prayer chain. When we hear bragging about what a prayer chain thinks they got God to do, wouldn't He have done it otherwise? Did He need to be begged to do it? Does any place in God's Word tell prayer chains to get a lot of people to plead with God for what we want? Or, is that a man made effort?

Am I right and they're wrong? No! I now see these things differently. I do not make it a right or wrong matter. That's God's business. After all, I have been wrong too many times to judge others wrong and me right, and He isn't through with me yet!

All these tools — What is God building?

Many writers give good answers to "What is God building?" They are true, of course. God is building His Kingdom, His Church, and His salvation. Those are true, but for us as individuals, as we seek His will, as we use His tools, as we live in Him, what is He building in each of us?

Oswald Chambers asked these questions, and they shepherd me through my petitions to God and learning from His answers Who He is, and who He called me to be.

Am I forming the mind of Christ?

How do I do that?

"I" can't. It is all about Him and what He has and is doing in my life.

Is God getting His way with me?

Some think God must force us to get His way with us. When you look at Jonah you see that God doesn't have to force us in order to use us. But He shows that He can and has. If you want to sail off in the opposite direction of a city awaiting revival, then God can and will send a storm, a crew of unbelievers who see God wants you for His purposes, and a fish so you can change your mind. Take all the time you want down there, but use the time to remember or come the first time to this: God is in control, and is using everything to grow His children.

God always gets His way with us, always, and maybe especially as we sin. God says, "Okay, I am ready to work in this area of you. To do it, I will lead you to a place of temptation. Satan will act as your tempter. I will let you sin, put the light on you, and then use all of that to build in you what I designed and have purposed, what is good for you.

Jonah saw the light in the belly of a fish. Okay, he might not have seen his hand in front of his face, but he came to his senses enough to obey. Did God bless him? Yes, God forgave Nineveh and turned away His wrath! Have you seen the light, or do you need to descend into belly-of-a-whale darkness?

The mind of Christ is more than knowledge. We equate knowledge with growth. Knowledge alone can't do it. Think. If knowledge alone grew us why would some of our great men sin? They have knowledge. They know what Christ did on the cross, and that should suffice for God to have all their love, right? Beyond knowledge, He guides our experiences to grow our love for Him. More than knowledge, God is forming Christ's Mind in each of His children.

I wrote about sin's being a tool, but it's more than that.
I wrote about God's plan for our lives, but it's more than that.
It's more than continuing the work He's begun.
It's all wrapped up in one great big idea: Christ = Truth!!
And consistency equals Truth. Christ was completely consistent like God is consistent, and to have His Mind formed in us would make us consistent, yet we settle for half-truths with

discrepancies or inconsistencies. Those discrepancies and inconsistencies must disappear.

So the Verdict Is In —
God wants us to have the Truth,
and nothing but the Truth.

Truth is God's favorite tool — because God is Truth!

The point is, everything we have mentioned — rebellion, lying, killing, adultery — all of it is labeled *sin*. Sin is a tool that God uses to show us consistency, to show us where our lives diverge from Christ as God's Truth.

What do I come to? Imagine that it is a crisp, cold morning and snow has blanketed the earth, muting noise, softening its features. You are a child again, and you can't wait to get out of the house after breakfast. School is out, and you woke up early because you were so excited.

You race through breakfast, run to brush your teeth, and hurriedly start putting on the layers to go outside, but you are not headed for sledding or building a snowman. You can do that anywhere at anytime.

No. Today is far more amazing, more exciting!

You are at Grandma and Grandpa's, the ones you wished for as a kid. Grandma finishes the dishes, gives you a hug, and you race across the barnyard to the shop on the side of the barn.

You burst inside to a warm voice calling out, "Close the door, little one, it's cold out there."

You close the door and stop. You take in the smells of differing woods, sawdust, oils to keep tools running perfectly, sharpened steel, and a heater over in the corner burning wood. The bright white light of sun on snow glares in the windows, mixing with the orange of the fire's glow and the lamps in the shop.

This is Grandpa's shop. Toys, furniture, and keepsakes have flowed out of here and under Christmas trees, next to birthday cakes, and into every room of your home.

Today, though. Today is amazing. Grandpa has decided you are old enough to learn to use some of the tools and together you will build the most amazing sled in the universe!

Ordered drawers and neat shelves filled with Mason jars of nails, bolts, and things you can't name are everywhere. Overhead racks hold wood: pecan, oak, and the mysterious mahogany, which comes from halfway around the world.

Today, you won't receive the work of others hands. Today, Grandpa is letting you use the tools, his tools to craft something that never existed before!

So, too, God the Father offers you His tool shop for making lives, building character, and enjoying life abundantly.

What I want most in this book is for you to see how God works in your life as you increasingly, humbly submit to Him. See God using any tool in you that He chooses. Learn how to use the tools He has given you to make anything He desires!

Stand on Your Victory

If you have ever read Aristotle on Ethics[255] you will see that he closes each discussion on a difficult ethical issue by asking a question, "What does courage require of us now?"

I point out one last Tool in God's workshop, courage, the opposite of fear.

A few years ago I argued a criminal case before the appellate court in New Orleans. To its three judges I said, "I realize that you will 'rubber stamp' the lower court's verdict notwithstanding the fact that its prosecutors grossly denied my client's rights. In their closing arguments they went far out of bounds, but one day others will replace you, your honors. Then as they sit where you sit, they will be driven to do what is right rather than blindly

---

[255] *Nicomachean Ethics* by Aristotle, 350 BC. Many great translations exist.

supporting our Government Prosecutors." (I had served for 4 years as one of those prosecutors.)

Those Judges had experienced how their system protected the Prosecutors many times, at the expense of the rights of the people. The hearing finished and as I left the courtroom, one Federal Prosecutor approached me showing complete disbelief that I had said what I said to the judges. He said, "Mr. Richardson, if I had said to those Judges what you said today they would have put me in jail."

> What does courage require of require of us now?
> — Aristotle

I responded. "They won't put you in jail when you speak the truth, and they know what I said was the truth."

I could share more stories like this, but let me finish this chapter. If we take these tools, all of them courageously, then God gives us three things to get us through our hard times.

He gives us:

Patience — The ability to persevere!

The certain knowledge that my hand is in His Hand, my heart is in His plan.

And He gives me a longing — to be complete, to be with Him, to have finished my race to His glory.

I wish you courage to prosecute God's Truth in your life no matter what the cost. Truth, as you may have guessed, is God's favorite Tool to use in us, because He is Truth!

11

The E. R. — Embrace & Renew

I want you to know, that based on everything you have read up to now, you must be wondering, "Okay, what now? How will God (not how can I) appropriate His plan in my life? I have read of His Plan for me, and It Is All About Him, but is there more?"

Well, let's go about it this way. Consider that you must make a trip to the Emergency Room, to the E.R.

The Emergency Room

Glass doors whisk open as you leave the night and enter, blinking at the bright lights. Immediately antiseptic smells, nurses hurrying, clerks taking notes, and orderlies flurrying by you make you halt.

Maybe you are walking in tonight because you lay sick at home for too long, got worse, and began to worry.

Maybe you are bringing a friend who brought this on herself by going into a dangerous situation and having her worst nightmare come true.

Maybe they are wheeling you in on a gurney because a drunk almost robbed you of your life on the highway.

Maybe they are wheeling you in on oxygen because a life of abusing your body has taken its toll.

But you have come to the big red letters saying "Emergency Room" in the night.

Here in the bright lights the EMTs tell nurses and doctors all they know and tests are ordered. One loved one stands near you as a talking nurse draws curtains around you and begins pressuring a blood cuff, removing clothes, taking vitals, drawing blood, and she asks you questions — so many, many questions: personal questions.

The doctors urgently seek to know what has happened to you. They must discern what happened in the last day and especially in the last hours. They must grasp your life in broad strokes because they are racing. They are racing to eliminate thousands, then hundreds, then tens of possibilities of why you are sick. This process of diagnosing a sick patient is exactly like opening up our lives to God's Holy Spirit, to the Great Physician.

When we enter the E.R. with aches, a fever, or trauma, all of those point to something else. Something makes us ache. Fever points to an infection. Trauma points to something drastically wrong inside us.

Spiritually, as we bow before the Great Physician in guilt, in shame, or in fear; God seeks to show us what those traumas indicate in our spirits. These indicators point to places where the Great Physician is ready to work in us.

As soon as our doctor arrives at a diagnosis, she embraces it. As she embraces it, she immediately begins to treat you for that diagnosis. Her embrace of that diagnosis means that she acts on your behalf, as soon as she is sure.

As soon as we come to the Great Physician, and submit to His Spirit testing us where He wants us to trust Him more, He then leads us to diagnose what is wrong with us. We can eliminate innumerable things God has already forgiven, and come to what He is perfecting. As we embrace God as our Physician, we embrace what He chooses to do in us.

The instant we embrace God and what He is doing — well, amazing things happen. Read on.

E. Embrace:
First We Embrace God,
Then What He's Doing in Us.

Everything in Christianity that can be distorted has been distorted. In my town, Tulsa, "seed faith" is distorted. Seed faith stresses our works, our faith, and our ability to manipulate God.

So, "is embracing God a matter of works?" Works in Scripture are an effort to gain God's favor. In distorted works —

- ✖ We try to earn something.
- ✖ We work to finally be worthy.
- ✖ We try to get some *thing* without needing God to provide it for us.
- ✖ We must feel as if we earned it.
- ✖ Because of our pride, we don't want to be indebted to God.

Embracing is a spiritual work in us. It comes only by what God grows in us. It is unnatural. We resist it. Satan resists it and distorts its value. It is a God-thing. You see, even as I embrace God while He does a work in me, my 'flesh'[256] rejects doing that. I fight against embracing, but God is greater. He is growing me.

So, when I enter a growth opportunity in my life and *can* embrace God as using any "it" that is happening to me,

- ♥ whatever "it" is,
- ♥ what I really embrace, is not the "it".
- ♥ I embrace *God as being in everything* in my life because everything that is in my life is there at God's bidding.
- ♥ I enter this spiritual place with a specific "it", but I then open up to *everything* God wants to point out to me.

---

[256] The Bible calls the struggling part of us, the anchor-dragging-us-down-part of us — our "flesh".

Why? I now know "it" will be used for my good, or He would not have allowed "it" into or put "it" in my life. So embracing is a spiritual work, a Holy Spirit work in me, certainly not me. Scripture condemns works that are all flesh and no faith. The point of any spiritual discipline is to focus us on God. It helps us embrace God and His Plan for us!

The ultimate "embrace of God's will" was foretold seven centuries before it happened.

> *He was pierced for our transgressions,*
>
> *He was crushed for our iniquities;*
>
> *The punishment that brought us peace was upon Him,*
>
> *And by His wounds we are healed.* [257]

When we are healed of anything, it is by Christ's being pierced as prophesied seven centuries before soldiers arrested Him. By His stripes we are healed. His wounds save us.

As we discussed earlier, here we continue unlearning. With one friend I had to unlearn two of my first reactions to an "it". My friend, Jimmy, was terribly sick and called to ask, "How should I handle this illness? I am swimming here — in over my head."

I encouraged him, "Embrace God and what He's using this sickness to do in you. Jimmy, He's using it to grow you more into His image."

He railed back, "You mean embrace the cancer?"

I answered, "No. I am not telling you to "embrace the pain or illness, but I am telling you to embrace God and what He is using it to accomplish in you, my friend."

He hung up. I had no idea how he might react, but I prayed for him.

Two things followed that may help you.

---

[257] Isaiah 53:5

First, Jimmy called the next morning to say, "I have less pain this morning than I have experienced in years." Unlearning time....

I refused to make anything of it. I replied, "Tomorrow you may rise with more pain than you've ever had, but the key is embrace God in all of this as He uses it all to make you more like Him."

Silence.

I went on, "Don't focus on the circumstances or illness, but get at what God is using this to work in you." Unlearning continued —

Second, I had to shake a temptation to be built up by Jimmy's call. You know how you play voices in your head? "Boy, Gary, didn't you help Jimmy get healing?" Only by clinging to this being "totally about God", was I spared that silliness.

So God continued to use it.

The next morning Jimmy called to say, "Gary, God used you to speak into my life. I am now re-thinking just about everything that I thought I knew about God."

Wow to God! How humbling it is to be present when He speaks to someone and encourages him! I saw Jimmy last week and he shared his healing with me. For the first time in years he is off all medication. Why? He embraced God in using the "it" in his life to do a work, to grow him. A WORD OF CAUTION: We don't embrace God in order to "get healing." We embrace God to have His peace, in whatever He is doing in our lives.

We are vessels used by God. When we insert ourselves into the spotlight, we start the Adam and Eve story again in us. It is no more about us than it was about Adam and Eve. Our glory is when God is in the spotlight, and all that's happening is about Him. Again, we don't embrace the "it" or us — we embrace God and what He is doing.

Jeremiah told a funny story[258] of how odd it would be for a clay pot (us) on the Potter's wheel to begin telling the Potter (God) what to do with it! When we function as we were fashioned, we are filled with fruition. When we center on ourselves as earthly vessels, rather than the One filling us, we lose our sense of His embrace! Remember: "we have this treasure in jars of clay to show that this all-surpassing power is from God and not from us!"[259]

From the Garden to today, when we embrace God and what He is doing in us (rather than embracing our selves), then God is magnified. The trauma is reduced. Consider this — what we fight against we empower. That being true, how do we weaken what we don't want in us? We embrace that God is using it, to make us more like Him. This is a WOW moment in our lives.

Forgiveness research and forgiveness counselors underscore this: we weaken something by embracing what God is doing in it through embracing Him and forgiving people.

Where does it say in Isaiah that *all* will be healed from the ravages of their sin? That wasn't so in Isaiah's day, nor is it today. God does heal a life "by His stripes" —

that submits to Him,
that embraces what He is doing,
that knows He works in us to make us more like Him, and
that He wants to heal.

Faith[260] is something all of us have, but in what did we place our faith? Is it in our healing — or in Him? Is it in our ability — or His to provide?

Listen to the prayer of a humble heart.[261]

> LORD, You have done all our works in us.
> O Lord,

---

[258] Jeremiah 18:1ff
[259] 2 Corinthians 4:7
[260] Hebrews 11:1
[261] Isaiah 26: 12-18

> *masters besides You have had dominion over us;*
> *but by You only can we make mention of Your name.*
> *You increased the nation.*
> *You are glorified.*
> *You expanded all the borders of the land.*
> *As a woman with child is in pain and*
> *cries out in her pangs,*
> *We have been with child,*
> *we have been in pain;*
> *we have, as it were, brought forth wind;*
> *we have not accomplished any deliverance in the earth.*

Back to the ER: When we try to act as doctors while really being the patient, we take God out of the picture and try to put us in His place. How's that working for you?

When we act as God, we botch our relationship with the Great Physician, and walk all over everyone else if they don't help our agenda.

We must embrace God and what He is doing in us. Then, God renews us, renews our thinking, and renews our minds. He is at work in you right now to do just that.

R. Renew.

Another thing God calls us to do is what the Bible calls "renewing our minds." Perhaps the best way to explain renewing our minds is to share something personal — let me share some journal entries with you to help you see how I discovered that I need, and I think we all need, constant renewing.

Paul talked of embracing God's plan to renew our minds this way,

> *Do not conform any longer to this world's pattern,*
> *but be transformed*
> *by the [continual] renewing of your mind.*
> *Then you will be able*
> *to test and approve*

what God's will is[262]
[What He's doing in you!].

My first journal entry —

‡ *I am really hurting this morning. (‡ Shows a new day in my journal.)*

I learned yesterday afternoon that my close friend of 45 years, who just last week told me he didn't believe that God speaks to us, has not been faithful in handling our money in our development projects. I have been weeping inside since he confessed that to me. Did I understand him correctly? Could I have misunderstood?

I have been in shock. I have trusted him over the years with my life and with my finances. I will lose several hundred thousand dollars if I understood correctly.

Where do I go? I find myself having to renew my mind almost moment by moment.

I can truly say I have no anger, just sadness, hurt, pain. These emotions could turn to anger and will turn to anger unless I get my mind renewed on the things of Christ. He is my Protector. Nothing can happen to me unless He does it or allows it. When He does, it will all be used for my good.

It is no fault of mine to trust a friend.

It is no weakness to trust a friend.

It is not foolish to trust a friend that has displayed trustworthiness.

---

[262] Romans 12:2

God! I am excited to see how You will use this for my good, for Your glory, knowing that You will. Lord, this one I have to work up to. Right.

‡ Another friend emailed me back — "Gary, after the shock and the pain rub off, and you can see clearly, you will see what God saved you from! It was God's time to uncover that negative force that was in your life! God allowed it for a time, now it's time to get ready for what God has planned!

"Go to Him, ask Him to help you renew your mind with forgiveness. There is really nothing you can do for [your friend] but forgive him. Forgiveness is God's gift for you, Gary. Forgiveness is not works. It is not for salvation, but just for the preciousness of your heart and your love for Him. Forgive the friend, Gary.

"One other thing, friend, I do know your hurt, disappointment and sadness. It will take awhile to sleep at night without hurting, awhile to wake in the morning without that "weight on your spirit" as you relive what you understood. It won't go away overnight. However Christ will heal your heart. "Time" doesn't heal — or God would be unnecessary. Time only allows us to stuff it somewhere, and one day it emerges as something so ugly. God, alone, heals and He is faithful."

I am so blessed to have friends who tell me Truth.

‡ Beautiful things have happened as I continue renewing my mind. At first I had to renew many times a day. Each day has required less and less until now, four days later, all pain, hurt and fear is gone. No longer am I pulled to become angry. Only now am I in a position to sit down with my long time friend and partner to hear his side, his explanation, without

> *needing to judge him or take issue. I need to schedule a meeting with my friend.*
>
> ‡ *Wow. What happened today in our meeting will be an example to me for life! I must remember why it is so important to renew my mind as often as needed in order to keep pain from turning into anger that destroys. I sat and listened. I heard him and learned that yes, there has been a big misunderstanding and that my business partner and friend had one understanding of his role and I had a different one. When we bottom-lined the situation, it really made no difference. Had I allowed my self to go on feeling wronged—had I stayed there, only destruction would have occurred.*
>
> ‡ *Following this situation, some really beautiful things started happening in our business that reminded me time and again how all this could have so easily been destroyed had I yielded to that which Satan would have liked to have seen. Thank You, God, for the work You have done in me that allowed me to take the direction I took. Not too many years ago it would have been ugly.*
>
> *[I finished the entry] —It's All, All about Him. Praise Him for revealing anything that holds me back financially. He is faithful. I am free.*

Once we understand how God uses *sin* to do His work in us, we need not fear what brought us into the E.R., in to yield to the Great Physician. It is in the spiritual E.R. that we again trust our loving Father, Who uses all things for our good.

Sin is a friend or tool that God uses to —

- turn us back to Him,
- change a negative situation into a positive one,

- convict us of wrong thinking,
- show us His salvation in ugliness.

On entering the E.R. we are given two options. Either we embrace what the doctor says and submit to the doctor, or we ignore what God, The Great Physician, is doing and go on. Jesus had the same two options in a garden, but His garden was not as lovely as Adam and Eve's.

No Jesus' garden was dark, lonely, sliding into evil's dire grasp as soldiers came to arrest Him.

What did Jesus pray as He faced His two options? First: "Father, if You are willing, take this cup from me." Second: "Not my will, but Yours be done"[263] Jesus chose the second option — God's will — hard, so hard for Him.

So, which is it for you? Will you embrace what God is doing, or will you grab your clothes and belongings and limp back out of the E.R. to go home sick, dying, and wasting away?

My second Journal entry —

I want to let you have a small look into my most precious gift outside of my relationship with my Lord — my relationship with Lanna, my wife.

> ‡ *As I trust His embrace* — *(‡ shows a new day in my journal.)*
>
> *As I embrace God, then I can trust what He's doing in me —*
>
> *I can embrace others; I can embrace what God is doing in others more like Jesus embraces them.*
>
> *In loving my wife, my real pleasure in loving her is to love her just as she is unless or until she chooses to change and does.*

---

[263] Luke 22:42

And if my beloved never changes that is okay. I told her that no changes would keep us from reaching the ultimate in our marriage, but we would still have far more than most have. I could not believe hearing myself say that — that I could and would adjust to whatever she wanted to give.

Now what she gives is what God brings forth in her for me, even as I learn to love her as Christ loved His Church,[264] messed up as the church was then and is today.

For my wife to grow to honor me, I will have to "let God do a work in her through me, while He does His work in her." I must love her first. I must honor her first. As I protect her while meeting her needs, I then watch God change her from the inside out.

Similarly, what does God do in our lives? He does a work in us from the inside out and grows us to the place that we want to honor Him. He loves us first.

I don't have that sort of love! I have nowhere close to that ability to love just as my wife doesn't, until God works in us. God must form all of those beautiful things the Bible says about love in us![265]

> *Love is patient,*
> *love is kind.*
> *It does not envy,*
> *it does not boast,*
> *it is not proud.*
> *It is not rude,*
> *it is not self-seeking,*
> *it is not easily angered,*
> *it keeps no record of wrongs.*

---

[264] Ephesians 5:25
[265] 1 Corinthians 13:4-7

> *Love never delights in evil but rejoices with the truth.*
> *It always protects,*
>   *always trusts,*
>   *always hopes,*
>   *always perseveres.*
> *What if I decided to try and change her by*
>   *—using fear,*
>   *—using shame*
>   *—using guilt and*
>   *—using punishment*
> using tools that are not His tools? Sure, but to what end? I desire to use the beautiful tools that God uses to work in us!

‡ *Well, the other day, I felt that she had not honored my wishes.*

When I realized my feelings, I also came to realize I couldn't expect her to honor them. Sure, we fell in love, and I put a ring on her finger, but neither of those change habits, change thinking patterns, change beliefs.

How could I expect her conduct, which has formed over years, to change instantly, regardless of her heart's desire to change? I couldn't expect immediate behavior changes and even more, I realize that I must "grow" her into honoring me. If she ever changes, she must first feel safe, honored, and encouraged by my love and patience, as I surround her with my trust.

How come I only now see that is how God works with us?

God is so unlike what I've heard for years. How could I ever bring my wife to honor me by using guilt, fear, and shame? God expects us to honor Him, as He works in us out of true love to form that honor in us.

Otherwise, there is no honor. Apart from Christ, there is no honor.

Could I insist that she honor me, and when she fails I punish her as couples subtly do? She may honor me some simply to protect herself—but that isn't honor at all. However, if God works in her as I honor her, giving her safety in love, then when she honors me it is true, and it amazes us both.

I remember that it was a lack of FEAR that allowed my wife and me to learn our wedding dance in such a short time after the instructor said it was impossible.

Now I finally see that when we first came to Christ pressed down by our weaknesses and failings, we surrendered the lead to Him for our dance in this world. And yet, even today I want to suggest moves, retake the lead, or help Him lead. Then when He is so strong and says, "No, I will lead," I get frustrated, angry, hurt, and worse, disobedient.

‡ What if our wives don't honor us in return for our honoring them? What I am learning applies to all husbands!

First, is that why we honor our wives? If we are supposed to be in our walk with God, we don't need our wives to "honor" us. We will honor them, period.

Second. God honors us in our honoring Him by honoring our wives. That is more important than our wives honoring us.

Third, if we truly honor our wives, then in time they sense that honoring them is not for us. They won't need to protect themselves with old, independent ways. They may stay there. But, if we mean that they don't have to honor us, then it comes down to one simple thing. Each man asks himself, "Do I love my wife? If I

> *love her as Christ loves His church, then she can relax into me, into my leadership, into honoring me."*
>
> *I suspect that the percentage of wives that truly honor their husbands is extremely low. If our wives never honor us, then I would say that we have failed them, not that they failed us!*
>
> *‡ With God as the Author and Finisher of our Faith, how can His sovereignty be manipulation? What could ever be manipulative about loving a spouse (His church), giving her safety? The root, the key to any motivation is, "Why is it being done?" If motivated by love, then it is not manipulative, but if it is motivated to get something in return, then that's manipulation. If moved by love, then it's done regardless of any response.*

We must ask the same thing of God's work in us, "Does He work in us to manipulate us?"

Never. It's to grow us. His love is "purpose" driven. Our actions are either "purpose" driven or "results" driven. We know God's actions are pure. Only the person doing what he/she is doing can judge his or her own heart/ motivation. The one thing we are not to judge is another person's motivation.

In the E.R. there is no Pressure.

Imagine that you now stand in the Emergency Room hallway and down the hall you see a frightening scene. You see a man in the hall. He is feverishly trying to stitch up a terrible, green, oozing gash in his forearm. Sweaty and trembling he smiles at the passing nurses and staff, acting professional while shaking with pain. His injured arm awkwardly dangles as he tries to sew it up with the hand he does not favor. Blood drips on his shoes and the floor, and dropped sponges and supplies litter the floor around him.

You are queasy, but you walk up to ask him why he is not in a treatment bay, letting doctors treat him, disinfect the horrid smelling wound, and sew it up for him.

He replies that he was called to be a doctor, and could have been if he had graduated college and gone on to med school. He is brilliant, so he claims, and he knows as much as anyone in the E.R.

You think he must be drunk or crazy. As you talk, you realize this guy thinks everyone goes to the E.R. and treats him or herself. He fails to see all the other patients being treated by doctors and nurses! He really believes that doctors are there only for advice. He is trying to convince you that you must do everything yourself! He is under incredible pressure.

You try to convince him to trust the doctors, and he argues angrily that it all depends on him!

Crazy, right?

Yes, and the church is filled with people just like him.

The church is filled with people seeking everything to glorify the self. They think Jesus is a great idea, but if anything is to really be accomplished, we must do it. These people are under constant pressure to perfect themselves like the man in the hall, but when we embrace God and what He is doing in us and remain in Christ there is no pressure.

What do I mean by that?

Does a pipe feel pressure from the liquid flowing through it, or is it aware of pressure from the flow? No. The pipe is dead, feeling nothing. Likewise God calls us to die to self. Translated, no pressure. We are the people getting healed in the E.R. because unlike the man in the hall, we trust the Great Physician. We feel no pressure.

Rather than people trusting God, we see God's children begging for funds to do their ministries for God's glory. They sweat and weep, unable to sleep over "their" ministries that are really God's ministries! Those ministers look like the man in the hall.

If that ministry is truly God's ministry, then I ask, "Why the sweat and tears? Why the anxiety?"

God has the power to build any ministry that He desires into all He wants it to be! And the minister? The minister is a pipe, through which He flows. Dead to self. If he has embraced God and His ministry, and is remaining in Christ, why the pressure? Instead, I see many a minister worry, anxious over what "this ministry's failure" will do to his image.

"God's will is God's bill" has been and still is true. Think. If God is using us for a purpose, hasn't He already made provisions for it? And if He has, must anyone then abuse, beg, distort or manipulate in order to get God's needed resources for His bond slaves to accomplish a ministry? I think not.

So a pipe, through which water flows, through which Living Water flows, has none of these concerns. It handles the pressure of what flows through it because it is dead to itself.

Embrace this. Let this flow through you! Here is God's ***Confidence*** in three translations —[266]

> ➤ Be confident of this, that He who began a good work in you will carry it on to completion until the day of Christ Jesus. (NIV)
> ➤ I am sure that God who began the good work within you will keep right on helping you grow in His grace until His task within you is finally finished on that day when Jesus Christ returns. (Living)
> ➤ There has never been the slightest doubt in my mind that the God who started this great work in you would keep at it and bring it to a flourishing finish on the very day Christ Jesus appears. (Message)

God said He would what? Finish what only He could begin when He saved us!

That's right. He said *He* would finish us!

---

[266] Philippians 1:6

No where does it say He needs our *permission*, our *will* (as most think), or our *cooperation*. If He did, that would make us gods of our own lives as some televangelists preach. Can you see that?

If it *were* left up to us and left to us to do the right things, what a mess we would have. Oh, wait a minute. We do have a mess, and this is why. We think it is about us. We think it is up to us. We all want to be the man in the hall, and we make a mess of ourselves and the world when we act like it is all about us!

We even say, "I believe all we have to do is believe." Think about that statement. How can we ever believe if He does not empower us to believe?

Christ's death on the Cross showed God's love, His love that redeemed us, also put all our sin under Christ's blood — past, present and future sin. All of it is under Christ's blood. That is simple. Read it, "How much more, then, will Christ's blood, Who through the eternal Spirit offered Himself unblemished to God, cleanse our consciences from acts that lead to death, so that we may serve the living God?"[267]

Embrace and Renew. E. R. Enjoy no pressure when we embrace the Great Physician's plan and work in our lives.

Add Remain to Renew —

After we embrace God and what He is doing in us —

After trusting the Great Physician and His tools to renew —

He welcomes, commands, adjures, and tells us to remain in Him. Please read what you can know as you remain in Christ.

> **As we remain in Christ,** God grants us **a view of eternal realities. He lets us** glimpse His plan.

---

[267] Hebrews 9:14

We can see that "our light and momentary troubles are achieving for us an eternal glory that far outweighs them all. So we fix our eyes not on what is seen and temporary, but on what is unseen and eternal.[268]

May He grant you according to your heart's desire and fulfill all your plans.[269]

In his heart a man plans his course, but the LORD determines his steps.[270]

Many are the plans in a man's heart, but it is the Lord's purpose that prevails.[271]

The god of this world has blinded unbeliever's minds so they can't discern the Truth, preventing them from seeing the illuminating light of the Gospel of the glory of Christ, Who is the image and likeness of God. [272]

God's Truth is Always Consistent.

When we remain in Christ, not our work, but God's gift, we see something beyond anything else in our world. We see consistency. God's Truth has a name — Jesus[273] — and when the Bible speaks of Jesus, it shows He was consistent.[274] Jesus was absolutely consistent, and, as such, is our standard for all truth. When preachers preach and teachers teach, they should, no they absolutely must, be consistent.

I weary of feeling sick at "the show" in churches. "Ministry's" entourages and games sicken me. I am completely turned off by manipulation, by hypocrisy, and how some "ministers" twist scripture for personal gain. All of that is false.

---

[268] 1 Corinthians 4:17-18
[269] Psalm 20:4
[270] Proverbs 16:9
[271] Proverbs 19:21
[272] 2 Corinthians 4:4
[273] John 14:6
[274] Hebrews 13:8

By God's calling, I focused much of my legal career to fight against such hypocrisy. Get a history of my cases and you will agree.

Some teachers teach good things, but fail the consistency test.

Dr. James Richards[275] is a counselor, who observed, "whatever takes hold of a new believer is seldom conquered." "Once a habit becomes habitual, the problem is usually there for life." That a Christian "usually falls into sin through ignorance or unbelief about walking in the Grace of God."

Okay. He then quotes Paul, "for sin *shall not* have dominion over you for you are not under the law, but under grace."[276] How can it be both? Do habits overtake new believers and hold those new Christians for life, or does grace abolish sin's dominion over us? Notice the words "*shall not.*" Legally, those are compulsory words. Absolute.

Again, Richards writes, "if the new believer would continue in the Lord the way he came into the Lord, none of these problems would ever occur." Richards fails to be honest about the battle, our obvious battle that starts in new converts' lives the day of our conversion. That is when the war really begins in us, the spiritual warfare.

None of us will ever win that battle in our own power, and the more we fight it, instead of resting in Him for it, the more we empower it.

God knew even this would occur: that Richards' inconsistencies would make for bad teaching. So God tells us to study His Word to protect us from inconsistent teaching. Richards gets it right finally: "when you came into this salvation, the Spirit of God did a work in you. Do you think that, now that you are saved, you will finish this work by your own ability? The answer is obvious. NO!"

---

[275] Grace: The Power to Change by Dr. James Richards
[276] Romans 6:14

How do we know that last part is good teaching? It sounds exactly like Paul's admonition to the Galatians! [277] We test any teaching by tracking it against God's Word.

He even goes on to say, "just as surely as you could not save yourself by your own efforts, you cannot bring about change through your own resolve. You are not saved by grace, then brought into righteousness by works."

I see many inconsistencies. We start to think like Dr. Richards (I observe that new believers with habits....) and we don't realize what a conflict we construct until we place our thinking up against God's Word! We fail to see our own inconsistencies, the places where we conflict with God's Word, where our thinking is incompatible with God's Truth, which is always consistent.

But this book is not about tearing down. I want to give you a whole new way of seeing what God is up to in you. He is continuing the work He started in you. Just as he said He would until when? Our day of redemption.

Again, not "if we say He can", or "if we give Him permission." We gave Him permission, to do everything the day He bought us. Part of everything that we gave Him in order to surrender our all was our will. We have no free will as so many preach. What we call free will is, pure and simple, rebellion.

We have sung a hymn for generations in churches titled, "I Surrender All." I smiled inwardly at times to think that most people singing are thinking, "I'll Surrender Some."

We gave God permission, to do everything the day He bought us. Part of our all that we gave Him in surrender to Him was our will. Again, we have no free will, as so many preach. Those "surrendering some" are calling rebellion free will.

---

[277] Galatians 3:3 "Are you so foolish? After beginning with the Spirit, are you now trying to attain your goal by human effort?"

So how to live in surrender? Where did Christ model how we surrender our wills? Prayer. He modeled surrender to God and to what God was doing in Him through prayers.

Prayer

Prayer has been my most difficult area to understand and grasp in my walk with God. I have asked myself often: "Why?" That is, "Why are there so many books on prayer when His Word tells us we don't know how to pray?"[278]

I hear so many prayers. I hear impotent prayers, repetitious prayers, and asking-for-what-God-has-already-promised prayers. Most prayers actually sound to me as insults to God. God didn't make me His prayer-grader, but even prayers from people I respect as spiritual giants often start far from Truth.

For example, a dear friend, a Baptist evangelist, recently asked me to pray that God would provide a friend of his the funds he needed in an up-coming revival through the offering.

I said. "I won't pray for that."

He asked, "Why?"

I said, "Why spend my time praying for something that God has already promised that evangelist? God already promised to meet his needs."

Often, I'm amused. Recently a pastor of great depth and wisdom, who I greatly admire, was pleading with God in prayer to "protect our missionaries and our college kids."

I sat in worship wondering, "God, does it bother You that we pray and plead for You to do so many things You've already promised to do? When we plead for so many things, does it make You feel like we don't trust You to do what You already promised? You already promised to be our Protector, so should we be asking for that or thanking You for doing it? God, does it

---

[278] Romans 8:26 also tells us the trusting remedy for this problem.

make You feel like we care more for those missionaries and college kids than You do? I don't know, but does our pleading and begging You for Your protection leave you feeling that You might just forget about them, and not protect them?"

Again, I couldn't help but smile to myself as he prayed.

As we embrace God and what He is doing in us, then our prayers begin sounding as if we trust that everything in our lives meets with His okay to be used in us to shape us. Please understand. I know what it feels like to start a prayer *far* from embracing, renewing, and remaining in Him. But the point of prayer seems to be that we *get* there, that we *arrive* where we trust in Him and His Plan — again.

I know God commands us to pray daily for some things like wisdom and knowledge. Praying for those has been my primary prayer for years since my conversion. Rarely, except those times when I am really

> Pay attention to my wisdom, listen well to My words of insight. Proverbs 5:1
>
> Blessed are you who listen to me (wisdom), watching daily at my doors, waiting at my doorway. Proverbs 8:34

hurting do I pray for anything else for myself, except to ask as god tells us to, for my needs, knowing that He has already said He would provide them. I remember when two specialists told me I would lose my left eye. On leaving the second specialist's office, I told God, "I don't know how losing my eye can bring You glory, but I do know that I wouldn't lose it otherwise. Thank you, God, for what You are up to in my life."

I didn't lose my eye. The doctors were amazed and my left eye in time went from poor vision to 20/20. Why, I ask, do we *beg*?

Why do we beg God for anything if —
we truly believe He directs our steps?
we truly believe He loves us?
we truly believe He is our Protector, and

we truly believe He guides us?

Again, I know that God commands us to ask Him for things, and I do. But those petitions are somewhat different than what I hear from our "pulpits." Yes, we are to ask for our daily bread, knowing we are asking to show that we trust Him for those needs, but not pleading or begging, as if maybe we think He won't provide otherwise.

Am I right, and those others wrong? I won't judge that. I can only say what goes on in me. I'm simply saying that I don't understand these people. I see these things so differently, and I think they are profoundly inconsistent when they don't begin or end a prayer in Truth. I wonder if they miss the mark of being confident in God's plan for our lives.

I won't make this a right or wrong matter. That's God's business. After all, I have been wrong way too many times to judge others wrong and myself right.

> *Embrace God's major act in history. He will present us to Himself complete.*
>
> *So He is using His tools to perfect us, complete us, and bear fruit through us.*

This brings me to the same point again and again — How can we ever, in and of ourselves, do anything righteous? Even in prayer, we are self-serving or worse, we pray to impress others in the room and forget that our prayer is to be to God not to impress others with how much we want them to think we care! Truly, It's All About Him.

Embrace "Busyness" — or not.

When we do not embrace God's plan to be renewed daily and remain in Him then we embrace other lovers. We prostitute ourselves with "busyness". Don't think the image comes from me. The Old Testament prophets threw red-hot zingers at our games and they called what we do when we don't embrace God and what He is doing, prostituting ourselves[279] or worse, chasing after wind.[280]

Even ministers chase after wind. I know many successful people, among whom a particular minister fills 19 hours a day with employee problems, editing materials, sermons, and researching his books. Now the world sees him as super-human, a one-of-a-kind man of God because he does all that and more. *He is busy*. He is "producing", but is productivity our reason for being? Is it all about productivity?

I wonder because I never hear him give God the Glory. I do not hear him say that God's Grace has washed him and prepared him for ministry, and I have never ever heard him say he was sorry when he wrongly judged people. Sound like chasing after wind? Does that sound like chasing after another lover — could his lover be himself rather than God?

We struggle with what to embrace, because so many, many gospels are offered, a bewildering plethora of false ones. How can we know? How do we sort through "busyness" and "bad gospels" to find and embrace the real thing? Let the verses on the next page guide you.

---

[279] Jeremiah 2:20; Ezekiel 16:15
[280] Ecclesiastes 2:17; 4:6; 4:16; and 6:9

The Real Thing — God's Plan for Our Lives

The Lord's plans stand firm forever, the purposes of His heart through all generations.[281]

Many, O Lord my God, are the wonders You have done. The things You planned for us no one can recount to You. Were I to speak and tell of them, they would be too many to declare.[282]

Commit to the Lord whatever you do, and your plans will succeed.[283]

In his heart a man plans his course, but the Lord determines his steps.[284]

"For I know the plans I have for you," declares the Lord, "plans to prosper you and not to harm you, plans to give you hope and a future."[285]

---

[281] Psalm 33:11
[282] Psalm 40:5
[283] Proverbs 16:3
[284] Proverbs 16:9
[285] Jeremiah 29:11

12

The Bold Frontier — Beyond "Scary" Things
Living in God's Plan For Our Lives

In a previous chapter I wrote of Jeremiah stumbling down Jerusalem's destroyed streets after having his image of God as his protector squashed and burned. That was scary for Jeremiah. It would be scary for any of us.

Do you remember that Jeremiah came back to God's mercies, God's goodness, and God's faithfulness?[286] That was Jeremiah's bedrock. It was his rallying point. It was his anchor. We all need such strength at times in our lives. Jeremiah reached a solid starting point to see the future God had prepared for him.

What Happens when we Embrace God as Protector

Trauma comes to us.
Embrace God.
Embrace what He's doing through His tools in your life.

Scary things happen.
Renew your mind.

Bewildering events descend on us.
Remain in Christ.

---

[286] Lamentations 3:22,23, and 25

And while remaining in Him, remember that even as others point out contrary evidence, God's Word says, "God is our Protector." From first to last, He is our Protector.

That said, nothing happens to us without first going through/by Him.

I want you to see a man embracing God as his Protector. His name was Ezra, and he was a lawyer—I like him anyway!

"Lawyer" to the Jews was one part scholar, one part judge for matters in life, one part community leader, and one part rabbi. Ezra was sick that the Temple rebuilding program following the Babylonians' destruction of it had stalled after the first wave of settlers returned to Jerusalem and Judah.

He was further sickened to hear that any excitement to know God in the people that returned had ebbed and disappeared.

Ezra prevailed on the Persian king, Artaxerxes, to let him return and lead a revival and finish rebuilding the Temple.

Artaxerxes said, "Go with my blessings — both material and well wishes." [287]

Ezra assembled Priests and Levites from around Babylon to return to Jerusalem and to lead in Temple worship. He amassed great wealth from the king and Jews for the rebuilding, and then he assembled everyone at the Ahava Canal, the jumping off place to strike out across the desert toward Jerusalem.

From there they would face a wild desert and Bedouins who ranged beyond the King's patrols, raiding groups such as this. Ezra's leaders gathered to ask him a

> Where will you be when you must say, "The gracious hand of our God is on everyone who looks to Him,"?

---

[287] Ezra 12:ff as listed in the King's letter to Ezra.

simple, wise, cautious question — "How many troops did you ask the King to supply us since we are carrying so much wealth?"

Ezra swallowed. He was at his place to embrace God as his Protector.

Ezra stood all by himself, staring at his leadership. All of these men were bringing their wives, children and grandkids. They had been Ezra's neighbors, allies, and business partners for forty years in this alien land. They trusted each other, and now — now Ezra had to tell them what he had withheld from these men, these leaders, these friends who trusted him.

He swallowed and told them, "I was ashamed to ask King Artaxerxes for soldiers and horsemen to protect us from enemies on the road, because we had told the king, 'The gracious hand of our God is on everyone who looks to Him!'" [288]

Some of their jaws fell open.

Some clenched their fists as their faces trembled and turned beet red.

A few old friends walked away gesturing helplessly to the sky.

A couple merely shook their heads in disbelief at Ezra.

They began to mouth their questions, "Why didn't you tell us?" "Why didn't you trust us?" but nothing came.

Ezra had embraced God. He trusted God as his Protector — whatever God was doing in his life.

God had challenged Ezra to put his actions where his mouth was. Ezra had told the king that God would protect them, and now Ezra was staring at the desert, which certainly hid bandits and raiders — and God wanted to know if Ezra truly trusted Him as Ezra's Protector.

Abraham had trusted God to protect Isaac and provide a sacrifice when he reached this place in his life.

---

[288] Ezra 8:22

Moses had trusted God to protect His people standing on the Red Sea shore when he reached this place in his life.

Joshua had trusted God's strong arm to deliver the Israelites and conquer the land when he reached this place in life.

David had trusted God to protect him as deliverer countless times when he reached this place in life.

Esther had trusted God to protect His people even after the genocide order was delivered to the furthest reaches of the Persian Empire when she reached this place in her life.

Now Ezra was in the place where he trusted God as his Protector.

Ezra embraced God as his Protector.

Ezra suggested some days to pray and fast there, and then they could set out across the desert. They did so. I imagine the prayers of those leaders, fathers, and mothers were terribly fervent! They set out, and cryptically, this is all Ezra has to say of the matter:

"The hand of our God
was on us, and
He protected us
from enemies and bandits
along the way." [289]

Listen to Ezra's explanation, you who have given yourselves as bondservants to Christ as Lord. Listen, you who handed over your will, and now trust your Loving Father's holy grasp on you. Hear Ezra's explanation of God as Protector.

"Though we are slaves,
our God has not deserted us.
He has shown us kindness in the sight of the kings of Persia:
He has granted us new life
to rebuild the house of our God and repair its ruins, and
He has given us a wall of protection in Jerusalem." [290]

---

[289] Ezra 8:31
[290] Ezra 9:9

Where do you need to embrace God, to embrace what He is doing in you? The Bible is unmistakably clear: God is our Protector. Here is a small sample from over a hundred verses proclaiming our Protector.

The Lord moves to protect you and to deliver your enemies to you. [291]

The Lord himself . . . protected us on our entire journey. [292]

David — "the Lord . . . protected us and handed over to us the forces that came against us. [293]

Let all who take refuge in You be glad;
let them ever sing for joy.
Spread your protection over them. [294]

O Lord, you will keep us safe and protect us forever. [295]

May the Lord answer you when you are in distress;
may the name of the God of Jacob protect you. [296]

You are my hiding place.
You will protect me from trouble. [297]

For the Lord will not forsake His faithful ones.
They will be protected forever. [298]

The Lord will protect him and preserve his life. [299]

I am in pain. May your salvation, O God, protect me. [300]

"Because he loves me," says the Lord,
"I will rescue him. I will protect him." [301]

The Lord protects the simple hearted. [302]

---

[291] Deut. 23:14
[292] Joshua 24:17
[293] 1 Samuel 30:23
[294] Psalm 5:11
[295] Psalm 12:5-8
[296] Psalm 20:1
[297] Psalm 32:7
[298] Psalm 37:28
[299] Psalm 41:2
[300] Psalm 69:29
[301] Psalm 91:14 Psalm 91:14
[302] Psalm 116:6

> Rescue me, O Lord, from evil men. [303]
>
> "I will protect the [orphans and widows]." [304]
>
> Holy Father, protect them by the power of Your Name —
> the Name You gave Me. . .
> While I was with them,
> I protected them and
> kept them safe by that Name You gave Me. [305]
>
> My prayer is not that you take them out of the world
> but that you protect them from the evil one. [306]
>
> [Agape love] always protects. [307]
>
> Our faithful Lord will strengthen and protect you from the evil one. [308]

As we remain in Him and He builds character into us, part of our character protects us.

> [God] guards the course of the just and protects the way of His faithful ones. [309]
>
> Discretion will protect you, and understanding will guard you. [310]
>
> Do not forsake wisdom, and she will protect you. Love her, and she will watch over you. [311]

All of us come to the place when God wants to prove He is our Protector and Provider. I remember one such time clearly.

Growing up in Texas, I enjoyed Denny Biddison as a friend. He was a year older and wiser and came from a good family. Denny tells in his testimony that God used my family's influence to bring him to profess Christ as Lord.

---

[303] Psalm 140:1
[304] Jeremiah 49:11
[305] John 17:12
[306] John 17:15
[307] 1 Corinthians 13:7
[308] 2 Thess. 3:3
[309] Proverbs 2:8
[310] Proverbs 2:11
[311] Proverbs 4:6

Denny was always studying, and found so many inconsistencies in our Nazarene teachings that he became a Baptist. Our friendship remained. In college, we lost contact, Denny surrendered to the ministry, married, and followed God's call as a missionary to Bolivia.

Ten years after we graduated high school, Denny surprised me with an unexpected visit to my office in Houston. I had no idea he was in Houston. We caught up on a lot since last seeing each other in High School. While visiting with Denny, God moved me to commit to send him $500 per month as long as he was on the mission field. I told him so, even though he wasn't there for money and hadn't mentioned money.

For the next two years I faithfully sent Denny my checks. It was sometimes a challenge with a wife and two children. Then I was offered what appeared to be a good opportunity with a new start-up insurance company out of Springfield, Missouri.

I bought into their company concept, based on what my old friend, the vice-president, told me. Unaware of start ups, I didn't know enough to verify the products. I sold more policies (52) in my first month than anyone had in a year's time making over $5,000, and this was 1969. Because of this, the company rapidly made me Texas sales manager and transferred me and my family to Ft. Worth. Three months later, I received a complete copy of the policy we were selling. Up to now, I had seen only the sales presentation. As I read the complete policy, I concluded that what I had been saying from the sales presentation wasn't at all what the policy said.

I contacted my friend, the company Vice President, who attempted to convince me that I wasn't correctly interpreting the policy. I listened because I wanted to buy into his explanation, but couldn't. I had truly hoped this would be a lifelong career move for me. What a letdown. I soon called to tell them not to send me my last two-week paycheck, as I hadn't worked, and wasn't entitled to it. On turning down that check for $1500 with that phone call, that left us $750 in the bank.

The next day I realized it was time to send Denny the promised $500.

It was time to face the future God had planned for us. It was time to embrace God as my Provider and Protector.

I explained the situation to my wife. If we sent the $500, we would only have $250 left — with the rent to follow in a few days. I felt strongly that we should send the money to Denny as committed. She agreed, and we did.

God was ready to show me again, that He was my Provider.

The very next day I remembered that my wife had been rear-ended in an auto accident months before. I told her that I thought the adjuster was in Dallas. I made some calls and he was. I left for Dallas to hopefully settle her case for $5000. I drove to Dallas, found the adjuster, and told him I had come to settle my wife's case for $5000. He excused himself to retrieve the file, and returned chuckling: "Mr. Richardson, there is no way I can pay $5000 on this case."

I don't remember any more of the conversation, but I drove home with a $5000 check. WOW. God had provided.

Two weeks later, I opened a letter from Denny telling me not to send any more money as he and his family had prayerfully come to believe God had released them from the mission field. They had awaited our check so they would have the money to come home! Double WOW.

When God showed He was my Protector, I could never have guessed how much He was proving with the same $500 that He was Denny's Provider as well!

I only knew that I could trust Him, especially as I fulfilled commitments He had laid on my heart.

Just like Ezra and so many others,
  in trusting God as Provider and Protector,
  in embracing Him and what He was doing,

God provided for mine and others' futures more than I could have dreamed.

The Ultimate Embrace

How does it look *perfectly* when we embrace first God and then what He is doing in us? God knew we would want to know. He left us a picture.

We see a picture from the Garden that shows us how Adam and Eve and all of us sin. God painted a perfect picture of His Son embracing the Father and what God was doing. Jesus' embrace is beautiful beyond words.

As beautiful as the Garden was, this desert was dark, frightening, barren, dry, and oh so lonely.

As poignantly present as God was in the Garden, He absented Himself from this desert. That was in His Plan for His Son.

The only constant in the Garden and this desert was the Tempter, playing his role with relish.

We pick up the story[312] of Christ's Temptation.

John, Jesus' cousin, had just baptized Jesus. God testified gloriously that Jesus was His Son and that He was pleased with His boy.

Then the Holy Spirit led Jesus to God's next thing for His Son: temptation.

The Holy Spirit led Jesus away from
- His family
- any friends
- any comfort
- any food and water
- any priests, preachers or encouragers
- to be utterly alone with Satan.

---

[312] Matthew 4:1-11, Mark 1:12-13, Luke 4:1-13

Scary, don't you think?

Please think about the temptations for a moment. They are unlike any temptations I have ever received, and I'll bet that unless you are delusional, you have not been tempted like Christ was either.

Why? Why when so many of our temptations are the same as everyone else's — sex, food, anger, power, money, abusing substances or ourselves — were Jesus' temptations tailored to fit only Him?

Satan thought his temptations to Jesus were designed beautifully to accomplish two things:

1) knock Jesus off of God's plan for Jesus' life and
2) make Jesus cheat, to use a short cut and use His "Godness" to accomplish God's plan. If Jesus had cheated, had used His "Godness" He could not have substituted for you and for me as a man when He died for us!

Let's take them in order. Satan tried to knock Jesus off of God's plan for Jesus' life. Please look at the third temptation with me. Satan took Jesus up to a high mountain, some have suggested Everest, where the two could see much of the world to say, "All this I will give you, if you will bow down and worship me." [313] Has Satan ever offered you the whole world?

Satan wanted to "help" Jesus reach the world. Satan could guarantee that the world would hear Jesus' message — any other way than God's way, any other way than in God's plan. Of course Satan had a small *fee* for his aiding Jesus, but that is not our point. Satan thought he could deliver the world,[314] and would have traded all of us just to have Jesus worship him.

Satan wanted to part Jesus

★ from His role as our slain Lamb,
★ from His position as our sacrifice for our sin,

---

[313] Matthew 4:9

[314] Much discussion exists in the literature, but if Satan absented his role as the tempter and accuser of men, it would be a lot easier for Christ's Kingdom.

★ from Jesus' absolute obedience to the Father.

Jesus answered with scripture, [315] which is a great way for us to blow off Satan as well!

Jesus stayed with God. Jesus embraced God and what He was doing. Now think about that — Jesus embraced God at the Cross in that third temptation, rather than accept a throne over the whole world! Jesus embraced God and His plan, rather than what seemed to buy Him an easier route to God's mission.

Jesus refused to be knocked out of God's plan for His life — even when He knew it included a cross! What a beautiful embrace of God and what He was doing! Hallelujah. WOW, that is so beautiful. He is worthy.

That is not Jesus' entire embrace of God. That was the third temptation. What of the other two?

Remember the first temptation? Turn stones into bread.

Remember the second temptation? Call down angels to protect Him as a public display.

We can turn bread into stone given a little time, but we have never been tempted to turn stone into bread. Why not? We are not God. We can't change the molecular reality of stone and transform it into gluten, carbohydrates and DNA in our bread. Only Jesus could. Only Jesus could be tempted to do that.

Why would that be important? Why would Satan tempt Jesus like that? What was Satan after in God's Plan for Jesus' life? Why was "stone into bread" and "angels when He needed" so important? They were supremely important because you and I could never do either one.

We could never rely on either of those in our own power like Jesus could. Those were both tied to Jesus' "Godness." In the first temptation, Jesus would selfishly have to use His ability to create as-God-not-man when we could not. Satan wanted Jesus to act as His own provider rather than trust God as Provider. In the

---

[315] Exodus 20:2-3

second temptation, Jesus could depend on His own ability to defend Himself, protect Himself rather than depend on God as Protector. So another way to see these is — Satan wanted Jesus to cheat, to take a short cut and not be like the rest of us. Satan wanted Jesus to truly depend on Himself, when we cannot. Satan did not want Jesus to trust God as Provider and Protector!

Jesus said, "No." Praise God. Jesus showed us —

For us to find God's provision we must trust Him, we must embrace God and His work in us.

For us to rest in God's protection, we place our faith in His character, in His love for us.

So Jesus, by not yielding to Satan's temptation limited Himself. Jesus said, "I won't use my 'Godness' to help Me follow Father's plan. I will use nothing that Gary could not use to follow God's plan except My obedience to My Father's Plan for My life."

I can be obedient when I embrace God. I can be obedient when I then embrace what He is doing in my life, just as Jesus did in that desert!

Think of it one more way. The Holy Spirit led Jesus into that desert, knowing that Satan would tempt Jesus to use His "Godness" and that Jesus would strip Himself of anything we could not use in faith!

Jesus embraced God in that desert, even when Father was using Satan to attempt to limit Jesus, strip Jesus, humble Jesus, and make Jesus like us. Wow.

In that desert, Jesus also unlearned for all of us a huge lesson.

Adam and Eve's motivation on eating the apple in the Garden of Eden has been judged badly, but was it?

They wanted to be like God, and isn't that the goal of all His children? Even now, we all want to be "godly" and "Christlike." Admittedly, their method, their effort to become like God was wrong.

Even today, how many have the right desire (to become like God), but wrong methods as they try becoming like Him by their works, rather than embracing Him, resting in Him, and letting Him be their beginning and end?

Jesus showed us how to unlearn all other methods in the Temptations, and He embraced God. Jesus embraced God at His Word. Jesus refused all shortcuts, and Jesus using nothing but obedience — looked so much like His Father!

How does it look when we embrace God, and trust what He is doing in us? It looks like Jesus going one-on-one with Satan and winning — even as Jesus got weaker, even as Jesus promised to use no part of Himself that would set Him apart from any of us! We grow in that strength and power as His growth in us brings us to that place where we are more like Jesus.

Did it *feel* like God was protecting Jesus out there in the desert? I think not. It was not until after Jesus at His weakest, dismissed Satan at his strongest, that God allowed an angel to come and minister to Jesus.

Do our feelings have anything to do with our embracing God, or embracing what He's doing in us? Not often, but what a power He gives us when we embrace Him, embrace God, and embrace what He is doing in us — and rest in His embrace!

Enjoy Him as He continues His growth in you. In doing so, you will find a joy, peace and love that you have never known. AND THIS IS A PROMISE.

THINK OF TEN PEOPLE:
CHILDREN, RELATIVES, FRIENDS,
WHO YOU WANT TO BLESS AND
GIFT THEM WITH THIS BOOK.
WATCH AS THEY GAIN A NEW FREEDOM IN
CHRIST, JUST AS YOU HAVE.